IT'S UP TO YOU!

**Why Most People Fail to Live the
Life they Want and How to Change It**

DR SCOTT ZARCINAS

OTHER BOOKS BY SCOTT ZARCINAS

Non-fiction

Your Natural State of Being
The Banana Trap

Fiction

Samantha Honeycomb
The Golden Chalice
DeVille's Contract
Ananda
Roadman

IT'S UP TO YOU!

**Why Most People Fail to Live the
Life they Want and How to Change It**

DR SCOTT ZARCINAS

DoctorZed
Publishing
www.doctorzed.com

Copyright © Scott Zarcinas 2019

All rights reserved. No part of this book may be used or reproduced by any means, graphic, electronic, or mechanical, including photocopying, recording, taping or by any information storage retrieval system without the written permission of the publisher except in the case of brief quotations embodied in critical articles and reviews.

Copies of this book can be ordered via the author's website at www.scottzarcinas.com, booksellers or by contacting:

DoctorZed Publishing
10 Vista Ave, Skye,
South Australia 5072
www.doctorzed.com

ISBN: 978-0-6485726-5-7 (hc)
ISBN: 978-0-6485726-4-0 (sc)
ISBN: 978-0-6485726-3-3 (e)

A CiP number is available at the National Library of Australia.

Because of the dynamic nature of the Internet, any web addresses or links contained in this book may have changed since publication and may no longer be valid. The views expressed in this work are solely those of the author and do not necessarily reflect the views of the publisher, and the publisher hereby disclaims any responsibility for them.

The author of this book does not dispense medical advice or prescribe the use of any technique as a form of treatment for physical, emotional, or medical problems without the advice of a physician, either directly or indirectly. The intent of the author is only to offer information of a general nature. In the event you use any of the information in this book for yourself, which is your constitutional right, the author and the publisher assume no responsibility for your actions.

Printed in Australia, UK and USA

DoctorZed Publishing rev. date: 15/09/2019

CONTENTS

Acknowledgements		vii
Ithaca		viii
Introduction		**1**
Part 1	**Prescribe Your Success**	**23**
Chapter 1	What Does Success Mean to You?	25
Chapter 2	Getting Past Yourself	41
Chapter 3	The Life Leadership Strategy	59
Part 2	**Life Leadership Skills**	**65**
Chapter 4	Life Skill #1: Who	67
Chapter 5	Life Skill #2: Why	73
Chapter 6	Life Skill #3: What	87
Chapter 7	Life Skill #4: How	95
Part 3	**Life Leadership Practices: Tier #1 Focus**	**107**
Chapter 8	Orange Diamond: Build Your Character	109
Chapter 9	Brown Diamond: Find Your Niche	123
Chapter 10	Yellow Diamond: Power Up Your Beliefs	153
Part 4	**Life Leadership Practices: Tier #2 Success**	**167**
Chapter 11	Blue Diamond: Refine Your Values	169
Chapter 12	Red Diamond: Retain Your Vision	181
Chapter 13	Black Diamond: Transcend Your Awareness	197
Part 5	**Life Leadership Practices: Tier #3 Elite**	**217**
Chapter 14	Green Diamond: Your Natural State of Being	219
Chapter 15	White Diamond: The Attitudes of Abundant Living	231
Chapter 16	Purple Diamond: Empower Your Life	247
The Last Word		261

For every seeker—may you find yourself in abundance.

ACKNOWLEDGEMENTS

I would like to acknowledge all who have been on this journey with me, some from the very beginning, others who have joined me later on. To my wife, Martie, a giant among mere mortals such as I, for your continual love and devotion. Leonie McKeon and Nicola Lipscombe, for your ideas, support, and belief in what I'm trying to achieve. Mike and Sarah Tapscott, for your positivity and for showing me how to attract abundance. Finally, my wonderful daughters, Zsa Zsa and Zenya, through you I learn more about love, life and myself every day.

ITHACA

When you set out on your journey to Ithaca,
Pray that the road is long, full of adventure,
    full of knowledge...
Always keep Ithaca in your mind.
To arrive there is your ultimate goal.
But do not hurry the voyage at all.
It is better to let it last for many years;
And to anchor at the island when you are old,
Rich with all that you have gained along the way,
Not expecting that Ithaca will offer you riches.
Ithaca has given you the beautiful voyage.
Without her you would not have set out on
    the road.

—Constantine Cavafy

INTRODUCTION

IT'S COMPLICATED

FOR MOST PEOPLE, life is more complicated than it should be. They feel as if life is a constant battle, a battle they are losing.

This isn't surprising. Despite the rapid advances in science and technology over the last six decades, life hasn't become easier; it's become more difficult and problematic. We live in a super-connected, high-tech world, yet we feel more disconnected and isolated than ever. In this age of instant information, we feel more overwhelmed and inundated than our parents and grandparents ever did.

It's fair to ask, 'What have we bought into?'

This overarching malaise and fatigue of life was highlighted by *The Metro* newspaper in the UK in 2000. Respondents to a survey on the London Underground were asked this one simple question:

Would you rather be at work or dead?

An unbelievable 55% of respondents said they'd rather be dead than at work.

Just think about that for a moment. More people would rather be dead than get up and go to work. Yet it's fair to say this hasn't improved since that survey was taken. With approximately 4-5 million passengers on the Underground every day, that's about 2.5 million people in London at any given moment who'd rather be dead than doing what they do for a living.

The question therefore remains: how would you have answered?

As a speaker, author and doctor, I've spent the last twenty-five years listening to thousands of people who are tired of feeling trapped in the same old routine, feeling as though their life is on hold. People grow up, go to work, pay the bills, get married, start a family, have friends and companionship, travel maybe once a year for a brief holiday, and before they know it twenty, thirty, even forty years have passed.

They start to ask themselves, 'What the heck happened? Why didn't I achieve what I wanted to achieve?' They look at others who have achieved more than they, and think, *Where's my success?*

It's worse when you feel frustrated and fed up, when you're stuck in a rut, or trapped in a job you hate. I know the feeling. You just want to finally do what you've always dreamed of doing and start enjoying life again before it's too late. Unfortunately, most people lack the knowhow to get the wheels in motion. They feel helpless and powerless, unable to change things for the better. They feel overwhelmed in what they think is required to make the change. Worse, they fear losing everything they've worked hard for.

You are not alone if you feel lost and confused. Or you feel as if your life is a myriad of dead ends with no clear path to take. You are not alone if you feel as if you're wandering through a labyrinth with no end in sight.

But it doesn't have to be that way. There is an alternative.

You can navigate your way through the maze of life. You can get your life back on track.

CLARITY

In *Alice's Adventure in Wonderland*,[1] 7-year-old Alice encounters the Cheshire Cat. Upon spotting him, she asks him which way she ought to go. The Cat ponders her question, then answers, 'That depends a good deal on where you want to get to.'

Alice, though, tells the Cat that she doesn't much care where.

'Then it doesn't matter which way you go,' the Cat replies.

---

[1] *Alice's Adventure in Wonderland*, Lewis Carrol, Macmillan 1865

INTRODUCTION

Although initially humorous, the Cat's answers contain a hidden solution to escaping the maze of life—*clarity*. You must first be clear as to where you are now, and then you must be clear as to where you wish to head. These are your two minimum points of orientation, 'here' and 'there'. In fact, when you include time, there are three points of orientation, the third being your future deadline. Without knowing your space-time location—your 'where and when'—you cannot orientate yourself to where you want to go and when you want to arrive.

Confusion usually arises when you don't know one or other of these orientation points, with the subsequent feeling of going around and around in circles, going nowhere, getting frustrated at your lack of progress.

In Part Twelve of *The Master Key System*,[2] Charles Haanel questions how much time and thought the average person wastes in aimless effort, and how much they could accomplish if they were to gain clarity and focus:

> *If you have ever looked through the viewfinder of a camera, you found that when the object was not in focus, the impression was indistinct and possibly blurred, but when the proper focus was obtained the picture was clear and distinct. This illustrates the power of concentration. Unless you can concentrate upon the object which you have in view, you will have but a hazy, indifferent, vague, indistinct and blurred outline of your ideal and the results will be in accordance with your mental picture.*

Lack of clarity is a common problem. It creates a hazy, indistinct and blurred picture of your life, and it feels like mind fog. This includes being as well as doing. You feel frustrated when you haven't become the person you thought you would have by now.

---

[2] *The Master Key System*, Charles Haanel, original correspondence course, 1912

IT'S UP TO YOU!

You feel frustrated when you haven't arrived at the place you hoped you would be after all the effort you've put in. Worse, you can feel trapped and stuck, despairing that nothing is ever going to change, as if your life has hit the pause button and is now on permanent hold.

For this is what it feels like when you're living in the maze:

1. You aren't being the person you hoped you'd be.
2. You aren't doing what you always wanted to do.
3. You aren't where you want to be right now.
4. You feel time is slipping away to live the life you always wanted.
5. You don't know how to make the change you need to free yourself.

The repercussions of this is threefold: stress, procrastination, and fear. You feel stressed because you feel lost and directionless, not knowing which way to go. You begin to fear that time is against you and that you will be trapped in the maze of life until the day you die. You procrastinate in doing what you know you should do, reasoning that it's all futile anyhow and nothing you do will make a difference, so why bother?

This mental anguish has knock on effects that take a toll on your physical, mental, emotional, and spiritual health. Your financial health suffers too. Relationships breakdown, your career doesn't progress, and the tic-toc of time begins to tick faster and faster.

Your confidence takes a hit. You doubt yourself more and more. You feel the burden of regret, which is a common companion through the maze of life, an imposter that constantly reminds you of all the mistakes you've made and how ill-equipped you are to tackle life's problems and break free.

In her book, *The Top Five Regrets of the Dying*, nurse Bronnie Ware documented the most common regrets that her patients

INTRODUCTION

spoke about in their last moments here on earth. In her experience, common themes surfaced again and again. Although there were regrets such as, 'I wish I hadn't worked so hard,' and, 'I wish I had let myself be happier,' the number one regret of the dying is this:

> *I wish I'd had the courage to live a life true to myself, not the life others expected of me.*[3]

We all want to do more than just survive; we want to thrive. We want more than just the humdrum of everyday existence; we want to prosper. But to thrive and prosper, to live a life true to yourself, you will need to evolve your way of thinking. You will need to evolve your mindset from the person you once were, and even from the person you are now.

You will need to become a Life Leader.

KILLING YOUR DREAMS

There was a time, however, when I didn't have the courage to live a life true to myself. When I was anything but a Life Leader.

It was a time in the mid-90s when I was a junior paediatrician, a time when I was living the life others expected of me. Unfortunately, I suffered because of my lack of courage to be the person I always wanted to be. I suffered physically, I suffered mentally, and I suffered spiritually. I had what I've now come to understand as a kind of soul sickness—*soulaemia*—a sickness of spirit that had physical and mental consequences, which mostly took the form of chronic tiredness, fatigue, and joylessness.

I wasn't even thirty, yet I had become profoundly sick with life; and if I had been on the Underground when *The Metro* reporters were asking their survey question, I would have given the same

---

[3] *The Top Five Regrets of the Dying: A Life Transformed by the Dearly Departing*, Bronnie Ware, Hay House 2011

answer as 55% of respondents: I would have preferred to have been dead than go to work.

The sickness I had was a familiar one: I wasn't doing what I wanted to do, and I wasn't who I wanted to be. I had a dream, and that dream was to be a writer. But I wasn't. I was a doctor, and I was frustrated and annoyed with life. I was frustrated and annoyed with myself. I was frustrated and annoyed with everybody, in fact, with the whole world. But I didn't know why.

I should have been happy. After all, I was a success, wasn't I? I had achieved what millions of people around the world could only dream of becoming. I was living a privileged life and I should have been happy and content.

Yet ever since I could remember, I wanted to be a writer. I wanted to write books. I wanted to write screenplays. I wanted to write for a living. I was the kid at high school who always had a book under his arm. I had a love of reading and a love of stories. I devoured books by the dozen, and one day I was going to write a book. I was going to be just like my favourite authors, Stephen King, Wilbur Smith, John Irving, and later, Paulo Coelho. I was going to make it as a writer one day. One day, when I finished high school.

But it didn't happen.

I was just a 'gunna', someone who was going to do something but who in fact did nothing about it. I had the dream but not the drive, and when I graduated from high school, I was accepted straight into the Adelaide University Medical School. I didn't want to be a doctor, I wanted to be a writer, but writing wasn't 'a real job' and everyone knew that doctors made a comfortable, safe living. So I spent the next eight years studying anatomy, physiology, pharmacology, microbiology, haematology, and telling everyone I was gunna be a writer one day. One day, when I'd finished all my studies and graduated from university.

But it didn't happen.

I moved to Sydney and completed my internship, still telling

INTRODUCTION

everyone that I was gunna be a writer one day. By now over a decade had passed and I hadn't written a single word of the book I was gunna write. How could I? I was too busy working, and with what little time I had to spare I spent socialising and traveling. There was simply no time to write. But one day I would. One day, when I could find enough time.

But it didn't happen.

In 1994 I flew to London for a six-week holiday and stayed for ten years. I found work at the Great Ormond Street Hospital for Sick Children, The Royal London Hospital, and other NHS hospitals. In 1998 I was accepted into the Royal College of Paediatrics and Child Health (RCPCH) training program. I began working extremely long hours, as well as studying for my specialist exams, all the while telling everyone I was gunna write a book one day. One day, when I passed the exams and became a consultant paediatrician.

But it didn't happen.

I was now thirty and had successfully postponed my dream of writing for over fifteen years, more than half my life. Not only had I achieved a double degree in medicine and surgery, I was now the Professor of Procrastination. I knew everything there was to know about fooling yourself and killing your dreams. When friends and colleagues asked me why I hadn't written anything, I always had an answer: no time, no money, no resources, no support, no knowledge, no opportunity. But I was still gunna write a book one day. One day, that was, when I had more time, more money, more resources, more support, more knowledge, and more opportunity.

But my favourite excuse of all time, the excuse I kept coming back to again and again, was this: 'I don't have a computer.'

I used this excuse for four years straight. It was so good I didn't bother with other excuses. It worked every single time. In the 90s, home computers were not staple items, and even though I could have bought one, I didn't. I made excuses instead.

IT'S UP TO YOU!

'So I can't write my book until I get a computer,' I told everybody.

Why nobody told me to just pick up a pen and piece of paper and start writing, I don't know. Perhaps they felt sorry for me. Or intimidated by my vastly superior mastery of procrastination. Nonetheless, the excuse of not having a computer kept the pragmatists at bay and my sense of victimisation brimming.

Because that's what I was, wasn't I? I wasn't just a gunna, I was a victim.

I couldn't help it if I didn't have the time to write. It wasn't my fault. I was a victim of circumstance. A victim of society's expectations. A victim of life.

What I didn't realise was that I was just like everyone else with a heightened sense of victimisation: I was a victim of *myself*. I was exactly where I was because of the choices I had made. Who I was, where I was, what I was doing, every single aspect of my current situation was because I had made the choices that created the life I was living. A life that I was now utterly sick and tired of and would rather be dead than at work.

Because up until this moment, I had not learned this one, vital fact of life:

> *Until you make peace with who you are, you'll always be dissatisfied with what you have and what you achieve.*

But I was gunna be a writer one day. You betcha. I was gunna write that book and, hey, maybe even another one. One day, when I retired and had the time and the opportunity to write. When I retired, geez, I might even splash out and get one of those computer things.

Then I had a vision of my death fifty years in the future and it turned my world upside down.

INTRODUCTION

LIFE PURPOSE

It was a cold and wet November day in London and I was extremely angry.

I had just had a verbal stoush with my senior registrar and stormed out of the hospital in a fit of rage. The fight had been over something minor, as they often were, but my sense of injustice meant I couldn't back down. My need to be right superseded my better judgement to let it go and not to worry.

So I told her what I thought of her man-management skills (or lack thereof) and fumed all the way home on the bus. I stomped up the stairs to my bedroom, slammed the door and yanked the curtains shut. It was barely 3:30pm, but all I wanted was to lie down in the darkness and go to sleep. I'd had enough of my job. I'd had enough of the doctors and nurses I had to work with. I'd had enough of myself and the relentless feelings of anger, frustration and futility. I just wanted it all to stop.

As I lay in bed, my heart thumping, my mind whirring, trying to find peace in the chaos of my thoughts, a gentle voice popped into my head: 'You know what, Scott? You could've been hit by a bus on your way home just now, and this is how you would have died—full of rage and bitterness and hatefulness. Is that really how you'd want to end your life?'

Geez, I thought, *you're right* (whoever the 'you' was I was talking to). *That would've been a pretty bad way to go.*

The voice paused, but it hadn't finished. 'So, when do you think you will die?' it asked.

I had turned thirty earlier that year and up until that point hadn't really put much thought to my own death. Even though I was surrounded every day by sickness and death, my own death was just not relevant. Not yet anyway. I figured I had about another fifty or so years of misery left.

About eighty or eighty-five, I answered in thought.

IT'S UP TO YOU!

Suddenly, *Bang!* I was transported fifty years into the future to my day of dying. I was both the thirty-year-old watching the events unfolding and at the same time the eighty-year-old lying on his deathbed. The curtains were drawn, candles flickered around the darkened room, and my future family were hovering around the bed—my wife, children, grandchildren—doing the death watch.

The voice now said, 'You now have five breaths left before you die.'

I took a long, deep breath in, then exhaled slowly, trying to fathom the meaning of what was going on.

I now had four breaths left.

After waiting for me to calm, the voice then asked the question that would change my life forever: 'How do you feel?'

Before I could even think to answer, I was swamped with a tsunami of venom. The hatred for life spewed out of me like pus from an engorged abscess. Revulsion. Rage. Disgust. Pure seething hatred. It was all-consuming. The hatred of those around me, those who had cared deeply for me. The hatred of those who had ever done me wrong, wilfully or by accident. The hatred of the life I'd been forced to endure. But worst of all was the self-loathing. The hatred I had toward myself was suffocating, a poisonous fog through which I struggled to breathe.

I now had three breaths left.

Overwhelmed and struggling to comprehend the revulsion and hatred I had for my life, I managed to gather my senses and ask my loathsome, future self one last question. I figured something terrible must have happened between now, when I was thirty, and the next fifty or so years. Something so terrible it had turned me into this revolting human being.

'What...,' I asked, 'what went *wrong*?'

What happened next is as vivid today as it was back then. That grotesque, older version of myself propped himself on his elbow and pointed at me in utter disgust.

INTRODUCTION

'Because you never gave writing a *TRY!*' he snarled.

Then, just as instantly as the vision had appeared, it vanished. I was now back in my thirty-year-old body, completely shaken. But I knew I had been blessed with the opportunity to change my future—to change who I was, what I did, and how I did it. I had been blessed with the opportunity to change my stars.

It has been said that the two most important days of your life are the day you were born, and the day you find out why. I had just experienced that second epiphany, and I now knew without doubt—with sudden *clarity*—that my purpose in life was to follow a different path than the one I was currently on. I had to stop procrastinating. I had to stop lying to myself. In the centre of my being, I knew who I really was, and I knew what I really wanted.

It was now incumbent on me to finally be true to myself and to be that person I was born to be. The consequences of continuing as I had were too horrific to contemplate.

THE LIFE LEADERSHIP IMPERATIVE

Your life situation today is the result of the choices you made yesterday, last week, last month, last year, even decades ago.

When you consider the current issues you face professionally and personally, and trace them back to the choices you have made, you see the link between how you had thought and the reality that followed. You also see the importance of changing your thinking if you want to manifest a different experience.

This change in thinking is a mindset challenge I call 'The Life Leadership Imperative'. It has the power to not only change your life for the better, but also that of your family, your friends, your community, the entire planet.

The contemporary definition of insanity is to do the same thing over and over again and expect a different result. The path to your prosperous future, therefore, is created by thinking differently—by thinking like a Life Leader. Sometimes you have to leave the mountain to remind yourself how beautiful it is.

Yet Life Leadership encompasses more than just thinking differently. Without action, any plans you've made are no more than just a wish. You have to walk your talk. Which is why Life Leadership is about being, thinking *and* doing, and why I define it as 'Living your Being'. This is best summed up in the motto:

Don't let life pass by you—let life pass through you.

As a Life Leader, you must be true to yourself and express the real you. You must find your Life Purpose and *live it*. In doing so, you will become a person of immense value. Others will value your passion, your endeavours, your presence, your cause. You will add value to whomever you meet, wherever you go, whatever you do, and you will do this not for personal or commercial gain, even though this will happen, but for the benefit of all. This is Life Leadership.

Life Leaders are therefore generous with their time, their self, their knowledge, even their money. They are beacons of light for others to follow, and by default they have impact and influence.

But it's easier to have impact and influence when you have absolute clarity on who you are, what you want to achieve, and how to achieve it. That is why the Life Leaders Club was created—to help purpose-driven people like yourself become the person you were always meant to be.

Which is the Life Leaders' definition of success and prosperity.

THE 4 LIFE QUADRANTS

So let's talk about success and prosperity and how it fits in with Life Leadership.

INTRODUCTION

We all desire success in some form or another. We all desire to be successful and to harvest the fruits of our endeavours, to be prosperous. Yet for most, success is elusive. For some it's tantalisingly close, just out of reach. For others, it's so far away it's nothing more than a fanciful dream, something only the lucky, talented or very rich get to experience.

But success is not as you might think. It is not just a result or an effect. It is certainly not a standard by which you are measured and held accountable. Rather, success is simply a process of being the best version of yourself you can be.

That's because of one simple universal truth:

Success is not a destination you reach, it's the ascendance to a new level of being.

Success is what you find along your journey of self-discovery, the riches you accumulate on your voyage to Ithaca.

Your success as a Life Leader is therefore the medium through which you can have a positive impact and influence on others. Think of your personal success in terms of context, content, and concept, the three vital factors of any organised endeavour. The outward path upon which you embark is the context in which you experience your life and all its unfolding events, including your achievements and failures. If your life was a play, the context is the stage on which you perform, with all its props, scenery, and other actors. Context is your *platform* on which you journey.

The content of your success is the accumulation of riches along your life journey—memories, emotions, relationships, money, possessions, family, career, and other achievements. Content is also the 'how' of what you do, the machinery of how you get things done. The importance of content—money, power, material possessions, social status—is that it is the *means* by which you can express who you really are.

IT'S UP TO YOU!

Which is the most important journey of success: the manifestation of the ideal *concept* of who you are—being the person you were born to be. It's who you are that counts as much (if not more) than what you do.

Success, then, is an inward and outward journey, of being as well as doing. The Life Leaders' definition of success integrates *who* you are with *what* you do, *why* you do it, and *how* you do it. But sometimes this is forgotten. Sometimes success is defined by only one path: either the journey into yourself (the ascetic, ethical, spiritual path), or, most commonly, the journey to outward achievement and reward (the material, rational path).

Defining your success as a Life Leader must therefore answer all these questions:

1. Who are you?
2. What do you do?
3. Why do you do it?
4. How do you do it?

Consider the 4 Life Quadrants in the figure below, *The Empowered Living Index*:

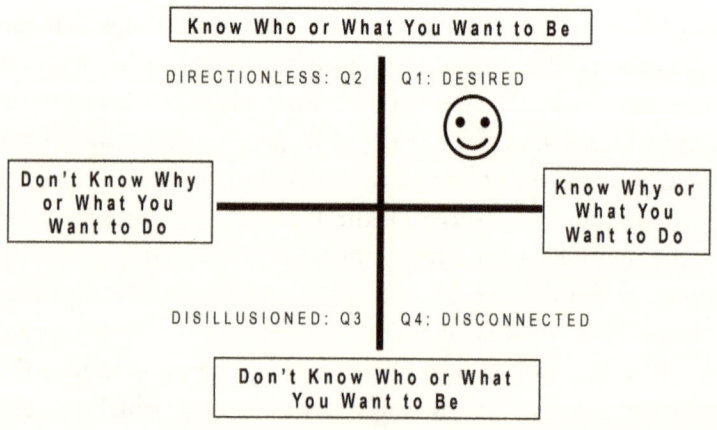

FIGURE 1: The Empowered Living Index

INTRODUCTION

As a rule, you will generally fall into one of these 4 Quadrants, but you may spend time in other ones too.

I will explain the function of this index in more detail in Chapter 2, but just to summarise, Life Quadrant #1 is the ideal or 'Desired' quadrant, your happy zone. This is the place where you are being who you want to be and doing what you want to do, where you find most happiness, peace and freedom—prosperity. This is the quadrant of Life Leaders who have attained mastery in their Life Leadership journey (refer to *Table 1: The Life Leadership Model*) and is the platform from which your life can really take off.

Life Quadrant #2 is the 'Directionless' quadrant, where you feel disorientated and in need of realignment. You feel you know who and what you want to be, but don't know why or what you really want to do with your life. You may very well know what you don't want, but this is not the same as knowing what you do want. In this quadrant, you feel as if you are going around and around in circles with no clear direction or focus of where to go to next.

Life Quadrant #3 is the 'Disillusioned' quadrant, where you despair with life and are in need of rejuvenation. You feel you don't know who and what you want to be, and you don't know why or what you want to do. In this quadrant, you can be so despondent you may feel as if everything is futile and not worth the effort. This quadrant can be a very depressing place to be, but it isn't the most dangerous. That's the realm of the next quadrant.

Life Quadrant #4 is the 'Disconnected' quadrant, where you feel detached from who you are and in desperate need of reconnection with your true self. I consider this the most dangerous quadrant because, although you might be outwardly successful, you have forgotten who you really are. You don't know yourself, and this lack of self-knowledge is felt as an inner void. You know you should be happier. You know the answer isn't money, power, or status, but if you're not careful, these outward trappings of life—wealth, power, material possessions, successful career—only keep you from being who you were meant to become.

Maybe for your entire life.

THE LIFE LEADERSHIP JOURNEY

You can achieve everything you set yourself to achieve. The difference between achievement and non-achievement, however, is not talent or luck, but mindset. Mindset will set you apart from the rest. It will lay the bridge to where you are now and where you want to be. It will give you the freedom and control of the destiny you seek.

Table 1: The Life Leadership Model illustrates the levels through which your success and prosperity can be achieved. It's a structured program supported by scientific research for getting your life back on track and keeping on track. Each level is defined in colours of diamonds, from the novice level of orange diamond through brown, yellow, blue, red to black diamond, the level of Life Leadership mastery. This 'novice to mastery' model will be the framework for your Life Leadership journey and is the foundation and focus of this book. Like the frame of a house, you build your life around it, brick by brick. Over time, you will have a built your dream home in which you create the life you want.

This model will be referenced throughout the book along with simple strategies to help you ascend the levels to at least the level of black diamond mastery (which equates to Life Quadrant #1 'Desired' in the *Empowered Living Index*). Each level represents the competent attainment of one of the 9 Life Leadership Practices. For instance, at brown diamond level your attention and focus will be on finding your niche. At blue diamond level it will be on values and the growth of your Ideal Persona. Each practice is designed to help you attain one or more of the 4 Life Leadership Skills: Who, Why, What, and How.

INTRODUCTION

It is designed for you to focus on what you see yourself doing, and what you see yourself being—and then living into that vision of who you want to be and what you want to do.

At black diamond level you have reached mastery of 6 Life Leadership Practices. You've become who you want to be, you're doing what you want to do, you've found your niche, you're living your life purpose, and you've mastered how you do it.

LIFE LEADERSHIP JOURNEY	LIFE LEADERSHIP ATTAINMENT				LIFE LEADERSHIP MASTERY	LIFE LEADERSHIP PRACTICE
PURPLE DIAMOND	✓✓	✓✓	✓✓	✓✓	✓✓	EMPOWER
WHITE DIAMOND	✓✓	✓✓	✓✓	✓✓	✓✓	ABUNDANCE
GREEN DIAMOND	✓✓	✓✓	✓✓	✓✓	✓✓	BEING
BLACK DIAMOND	✓	✓	✓	✓	✓	TRANSCEND
RED DIAMOND	✓	✓	✓	✓	✗	VISION
BLUE DIAMOND	✓	✓	✓	✗	✗	VALUES
YELLOW DIAMOND	✓	✓	✗	✗	✗	BELIEF
BROWN DIAMOND	✓	✗	✗	✗	✗	NICHE
ORANGE DIAMOND	✗	✗	✗	✗	✗	CHARACTER

TABLE 1:   The Life Leadership Model

When you have attained black diamond mastery, your life will look like this:

1. The Joy of Life: you will feel a permanent sense of happiness and enthusiasm that comes from the rejuvenation of your Inner Power.
2. Complete Confidence: you will feel a profound conviction and inner confidence that comes from the realignment with your Life Purpose.
3. Immeasurable Value: you will feel a sense of total self-acceptance, respect, and worth that comes from the reconnection with your Ideal Persona.
4. Peace of Mind: you will feel a deep calmness and inner harmony that comes from the attainment of higher levels of awareness and perspective.
5. Ultimate Freedom: you will feel an unlimited sense of freedom that comes from the implementation of the Life Leaders mindset.

You will have progressed from where you are now, to where you want to be—a transcendence from your current 'you' to your ideal 'you'.

Figure 2: The Life Leadership Wheel illustrates how the whole Life Leadership process works.

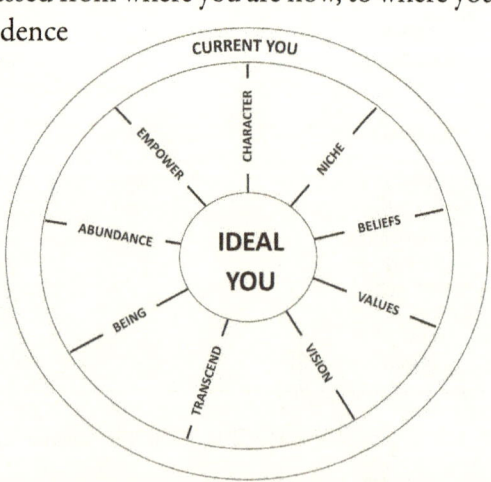

FIGURE 2:   The Life Leadership Wheel

INTRODUCTION

It is a continual work in progress. *You* are a continual work in progress. Improvement never stops. The Life Leadership Wheel is always turning, always in motion, always progressing toward the manifestation of your ideal self.

YOUR LIFE, YOUR CHOICE

We all want to prosper, but one of the biggest fears we face is that the change we need to make is so big it's overwhelming and unobtainable. Furthermore, will our partner stand for it? Will we lose everything we've worked hard for over the years?

I understand these concerns, but even though change can be hard and frightening, my philosophy is for small changes of mindset that reap huge benefits to your life and relationships at home and at work. The Life Leadership journey isn't about giving up everything and becoming a new person at all, just a better version of yourself.

As Bruce Lee said:

> *There are no limits. There are only plateaus, and you must not stay there; you must go beyond them.*

At times you don't just go beyond your limitations, you have to smash through them. One of my self-imposed limitations used to be selling, especially cold call selling. I used to hate making phone calls to prospective businesses to sell my presentations and courses, so much so my business just staggered along. I wanted somebody else to do the dirty work, but nobody else was going to. Only I could make the calls, but I didn't. I preferred to write the books and deliver the presentations. I didn't want to pick up the phone and speak to strangers. I felt I was useless at selling. I felt I was my own worst enemy.

In fact, I was. But not how I thought I was. I was my own worst enemy because I had put a glass ceiling above my head that I couldn't penetrate. Not with my current mindset anyhow.

It was only later, when circumstances forced me to consider how my limiting beliefs were suffocating my business ambitions, that I stared down my fear of cold calling (which was really a fear of rejection) and made my first call.

The call, in fact, didn't turn out that well. But it didn't matter. I'd made the call and smashed through my limitations. Now, if those same fears resurface, I always remember that I'd done it before and can do it again.

If you're facing similar self-imposed limitations, only you can go beyond yourself and succeed and prosper. It's your life, your choice. If the stars are your destination, this book is going to show you how to build your stairway to them. Having the dream is one thing, but without knowing how to put into place the necessary steps to reach them, then the chances are they'll always remain out of reach.

This book, then, is your go-to manual if:

1. You want *real* success and prosperity.
2. You *desire* to achieve something you've never achieved before.
3. You *seek* to become what you always wanted to become.

However, this book is not about waving a magic wand and expecting all your dreams to come true. This book is not going to:

1. Maintain the status quo—you will need to get comfortable with being uncomfortable because rising through the levels of Life Leadership means shedding old habits and developing new ones. Which can feel awkward and unpleasant at first, but that's where the true growth and prosperity is to be achieved.

INTRODUCTION

2. Make you a millionaire and set you up financially for life—you may well do so in your Life Leadership journey, but the success and prosperity you will achieve is more permanent and lifelong because it will come from your inner world, which is constant and always with you no matter what happens in the outside world.

3. Make all your problems go away and never come back—rather, it will give you all the tools you need to *overcome* and resolve the problems you currently face, as well as the unforeseen challenges that will most certainly arise as you journey through the levels of Life Leadership.

In my book, *Your Natural State of Being*, I explained how you already have what you're looking for—how you already have all the joy, security, acceptance, peace, and freedom you seek. In this book, I will go one step further. I will show you how to rejuvenate your personal and professional life by realigning with your purpose, passion and values so that you can find direction and live the life you always wanted without feeling overwhelmed or fearing change.

As the Chinese proverb says, 'The journey of a thousand miles begins with the first step.' Your journey to success and prosperity begins when you open the door to your own power.

This book is how you open that door to your inner power. For too long you have kept your power locked away. For too long your potential has remained untapped and unfulfilled. When you align who you are with what you want and how to achieve it, your intentions manifest into reality. The more precise your being, thoughts, and action are in alignment—the more *harmonious* you are with yourself, your purpose, and your behaviour—the more likely and the more speedily your success and prosperity is realised.

It's now up to you. If you want to discover the world of

IT'S UP TO YOU!

infinite possibilities that await you, join me on the journey to Life Leadership prosperity.

But if the imposter in your head is causing you to doubt your chances of success, or telling you that you don't deserve to live a life of prosperity, then let me counter that with a parable.

The Parable of the Dog goes like this. One evening a young man walked into his friend's kitchen and saw a dog curled up in the corner, whimpering in pain.

'What's wrong with your dog?' he asked his friend.

'Oh, he has sat on a nail poking through the floorboards.'

The young man scratched his head. 'So, why doesn't he move?'

'Because,' his friend explained, 'it doesn't hurt *enough*.'

My question to you, then, is: Are you just putting up with the pain of everyday life because it doesn't hurt enough for you to do anything different and move forward?

Unfortunately, it's common for people (and dogs) to put up with things that aren't desirable. Are you one of them? What will it take for you to say, 'Enough is enough!'

Let me show you something that might motivate you to move forward. I would like you to do a simple piece of mathematics.

First, subtract your current age from the number 85 (i.e. 85 − your age = X?). At the time of writing, my age is 50, so my answer is 35.

Next, multiply your answer by 5 (i.e. X x 5 = Y?). For me, 35 x 5 is 175.

Lastly, add a zero to your answer. For me, my answer is 1750.

Now take a good look at your answer. That number is the *total number of weeks you have left to live*.[4]

Are you motivated yet? Does it hurt enough to get up and get moving?

It's up to you.

---

[4] Assuming that 85 years is the average lifespan and using 50 as the number of weeks in a single year.

PART I

PRESCRIBE YOUR SUCCESS

1 WHAT DOES SUCCESS MEAN TO YOU?

THE SECRET TO SUCCESS

Is there a secret to success?

Not particularly. If anything, if it is a secret, it's an open secret. Unfortunately, in our busy lives, this open secret gets overlooked. This secret isn't hidden, known only by a special few who got lucky or who are privileged. It's a secret available to everyone. It just gets missed in the busyness of our everyday lives. We can't see the trees from the forest. We can't see the cause from the effect.

But here's the secret most people don't know. Note it down. Memorise it. Do whatever you need to remember it because it has the potential to change your life from this moment on:

> *The secret to success reveals itself when you ask the right questions.*

Life Leaders know this. They know their success depends on their ability to ask the right questions.

THE GAME OF LIFE

We will discuss the right questions to ask soon, but before we do it's important to note that the process, not the result, is where your success and prosperity will be found. Perfection, as they say, is in the process.

That's why knowing the rules of the game you're playing are so important. They help you get to where you want to go. When you

IT'S UP TO YOU!

focus on the process, the *how*, the results you're after will take care of themselves. When you focus only on the outcome, the result, it's easy to forget the process of how to achieve that outcome. Of course, it's important not to lose sight of the intended goal; your goal keeps you orientated, heading in the right direction. But one eye should also be kept on the mechanics of getting things done.

On the football field, the team that succumbs to scoreboard pressure can lose sight of what it needs to do to win. The team's structure starts to unravel, the players forget the basics of how to defend and attack, teamwork gets subjugated for individual glory, and invariably the team gets overrun by the opposition and loses.

The team that doesn't lose focus on its structure and processes, however much pressure they find themselves under, usually win more games than they lose and rise to the top of the league table. When they get the fundamentals right, when they get the basics of the game right, success invariably looks after itself.

The same principles hold true with your personal brand of success. In fact, the game of success and prosperity is called the Game of Life. It is a wonderful game of giving and receiving, and it has rules by which you must abide if you wish to play the game. But it also has penalties for not following the rules, which usually begins with a capital 'F' and ends in 'ailure'.

Take, for instance, the universe in which we live. It has set laws of physics, such as the Law of Gravity and the First Law of Energy.[5] Without these universal laws, physical life as we know it probably wouldn't exist.

Other minor rules also exist for what we can and cannot do. Traffic rules, for example, keep traffic in one direction to one side of the road and limited to a certain speed. Board games, card games, and other games have rules by which the game can be played. Just as the universal laws provide the framework in

---

[5] The First Law of Energy states that all energy in the universe is a constant, that energy cannot be made or destroyed, only changed in form.

which physical life can flourish, game rules provide the terms of engagement in which the games we play can proceed.

Similarly, the Game of Life has a set of rules by which your personal brand of success can be achieved. There are rules of engagement. There are set processes. Follow these rules, follow these processes, and the Game of Life can be won, success and prosperity can be yours.

If not, disorder will set in. Failure will be the norm.

RULES OF THE GAME

In presenting you with these rules, keep in mind that they should be treated as adaptable, personalised guidelines and not rigid bureaucratic processes. If you are a student of life, you will recognise these rules and advice. I haven't invented something revolutionary. Just as scientists describe patterns in the way the universe works with mathematical formulas, I've observed a pattern in how life works and put a formula to it.

The rules of the Game of Life are, in fact, rather easy. Anybody can use them to achieve their own personal brand of success. The rules are tools to apply to your own life situation and adapt accordingly. It's not rocket science, but these rules will help you get beyond the stratosphere to your stars.

Here, then, is the open secret, the rules to which you can play the Game of Life and be a success at whatever you commit to:

THE 3 GOLDEN RULES:

Rule #1: *Define Who You Are*
Rule #2: *Determine What You Want*
Rule #3: *Design How to Achieve It*

IT'S UP TO YOU!

These '3 Golden Rules'[6] are the keys to opening the door to Life Quadrant #1 on the Empowered Living Index, the quadrant of Life Leadership mastery. Rule #1 reconnects you with your Ideal Persona. Rule #2 realigns you with your Life Purpose. Rule #3 rejuvenates your Inner Power. They basically follow the adage:

You've got to <u>be</u> before you can do, and you've got to <u>do</u> before you can have.

Be first. Do second. Have third. That's the sequence of success, and this is how the process works:

- -> Defining who you are unlocks the best vision and biggest version of yourself—*your ideal you.*
- -> Determining what you want maps the pathway of your journey from where you are now to where you want to be—*your vision process.*
- -> Designing how you achieve it results in the materialisation of your intent—*the manifestation of your personal brand of success.*

Later, we will discuss the 3 Golden Rules in terms of developing your 4 Life Leadership Skills:

- ♦ Life Skill #1–Who
- ♦ Life Skill #2–Why
- ♦ Life Skill #3–What
- ♦ Life Skill #4–How

For now, the rules of the Game of Life can be represented like this:

---

[6] There is a fourth, silent rule—*Rule #4: Deliver It.* This rule simply says that you need to take action on the first 3 Rules of Defining, Determining, and Designing. You need to do what you say you'll do. You need to put your plans into action. You need to maintain the habit of doing in order to deliver the success you want.

WHAT DOES SUCCESS MEAN TO YOU?

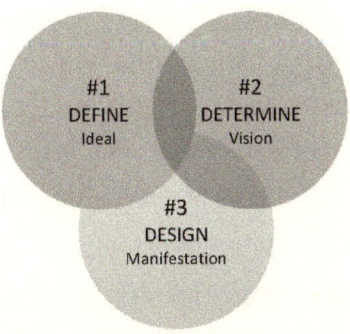

FIGURE 3: Rules of The Game of Life—
Define, Determine, Design

Delving deeper, we can identify a few more points of detail at the intersections where these three rules bridge and overlap. These are the 3 Life Leadership Axes: I Am, I Will, I Can.

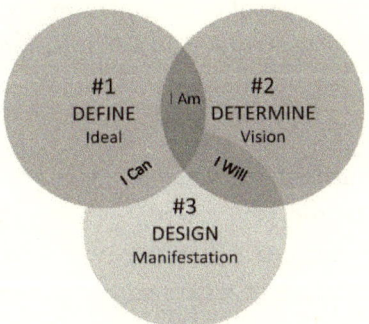

FIGURE 4: Life Leadership Axes—
I Am, I Will, I Can

#1 Axis–I Am

The first overlap is where Rule #1: Define Who You Are bridges with Rule #2: Determine What You Want, where your Ideal Persona merges with your visualisation. Here you develop a deep understanding of your essential *beingness*, your 'I Am' axis. This you do on three tiers of Life Leadership (which, along with the Life Leadership Practices, will be discussed in greater depth in the following chapters):

- Tier #1: The *character* of your 'I Am'.
- Tier #2: The *values* of your 'I Am'.
- Tier #3: The state of *being* of your 'I Am'.

The importance of this is the development of your character, values, and being in alignment with your Ideal Persona. Not what somebody else has told you who you should be; anything other than being yourself won't get the results you're after.

It's critical, therefore, to get absolute clarity on the ideal person you wish to become. You don't need to get too complicated here. Your idea of your ideal self, the self you want to grow into, can be as simple as three character strengths you admire, three values you believe in, and three states of being you wish to embody.

The simpler you know your ideal self, the easier it is to express it.

#2 Axis–I Will

Your 'I Am' is your first reference point in your Life Leadership journey. It leads to the next reference point, the second overlap where Rule #2: Determine What You Want bridges with Rule #3: Design How to Achieve It, where your visualisation merges with your manifestation. Here you develop a deep understanding of your inner drive and *intention*, what I call your 'I Will' axis.

As with your 'I Am', you do this on three tiers of Life Leadership:

- Tier #1: Identifying your THING and finding your *niche*.
- Tier #2: Retaining alignment of your *vision*, values, and life purpose.
- Tier #3: Harnessing abundance with the *Attitudes of Abundant Living*.

WHAT DOES SUCCESS MEAN TO YOU?

Without clarity of who you are, you cannot get clarity of what you intend to do. That's why your 'I Am' precedes your 'I Will'. Defining who you are with clarity allows you to clearly visualise and determine what you want to do.

#3 Axis–I Can

Likewise, having clarity of purpose leads to clarity of how to do it. When you are clear on what you want to achieve, you get clearer on how you can go about it. Your second reference point, your 'I Will', therefore precedes your third reference point, your 'I Can'. Which is found at the overlap where Rule #3: Design How to Achieve It bridges with Rule #1: Define Who You Are, where your manifestation merges with your Ideal Persona.

Here you develop a deep understanding of your own *innate power*. As with your 'I Am' and 'I Will', you do this on three tiers of Life Leadership:

- Tier #1: Identifying self-limiting beliefs and establishing *empowering beliefs*.
- Tier #2: Transcending your *awareness* to new levels.
- Tier #3: Overcoming fears and establishing *empowering behaviours*.

Integral to experiencing your innate power is the understanding that thoughts precede emotions and actions. How you think is how you feel is how you behave, and so to establish positive emotion and behaviour patterns you first need to establish positive thought patterns. Self-limiting beliefs lead to self-limiting attitudes and self-sabotaging behaviours. Empowered beliefs lead to self-determining attitudes and self-empowering behaviours.

Those who have achieved Life Leadership mastery have mastered control of how they think, feel and behave.

IT'S UP TO YOU!

THE DIAMOND TRIANGLE

For centuries, scientists have striven to develop the ultimate mechanical system, a self-perpetuating process that once set into motion requires no further input of energy to keep it operating. The ideal is to create a system that can keep going forever, like a clock that never stops.

Unfortunately, such a system has yet to be developed. External forces like gravity, magnetism, and friction sap energy and disrupt any efforts to build this ideal system. Additional energy is always required to replenish the depleted energy and keep it moving, which is why clocks need batteries and watches need winding.

The three axis points of 'I Am, I Will, I Can' triangulate with one another in an enclosed system that is as close to self-perpetuating as any system that has been created to date. Once you have created your own personal system using the 3 Golden Rules and put it into motion, all that's required is to input a little energy to keep the system moving. You need to keep your eye on the ball and not let the system slowly run out of energy.

That's your job, but once the system is running smoothly, it will provide you with the means to ascend the levels of Life Leadership, like an escalator taking you up the levels of a department store. I call this self-perpetuating system *The Diamond Triangle*.

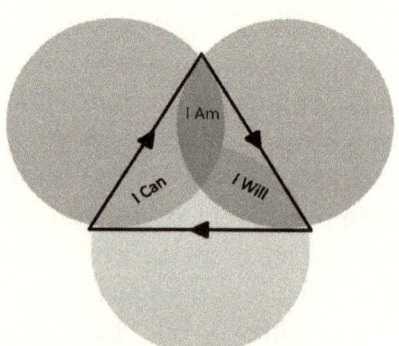

FIGURE 5: The Diamond Triangle—
Self-Perpetuating System

WHAT DOES SUCCESS MEAN TO YOU?

In nature, diamonds are crystallised forms of pure carbon that have been created by intense pressure in the mantle of the earth. The word 'diamond' is derived from the Greek word, *adámas,* which means unbreakable and untamed. The 3 Golden Rules form the three sides of The Diamond Triangle, within which are housed your three axis points of being, intent, and power—I Am, I Will, I Can.

When each rule is linked by a thread of *purpose*, a definitive aim, their power is intensified. Your purpose is your reason for being who you are, doing what you do, and how you do it. Like a magnifying glass focussing rays of sunlight, each rule focuses the aim of your purpose toward a focal point in the centre of the triangle. But because The Diamond Triangle is synergistic, its effect is greater than the sum of its parts, or in this case its rules. So when these rules align, this synergy crystallises in the centre of the triangle as a precious gem, a diamond—your personal brand of success.

This, then, is The Diamond Triangle:

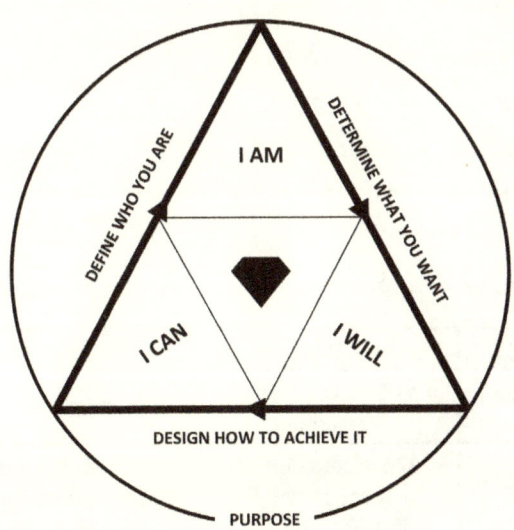

FIGURE 6: The Diamond Triangle—
Design, Determine, Define

Each rule of *defining* yourself, *determining* what you want, and *designing* how to achieve it can be used independently of each other, and moderate success attained. But it's when they are used in synergy with each other that your full potential is realised. Your purpose is integral to that. It strengthens your commitment and dedication to your success, and when combined with action, you have the power to turn your failures into victories and to manifest your personal brand of success.

The Diamond Triangle is how you reach Life Leadership mastery.

THE 4 TENETS OF SUCCESS

Success can mean a lot of different things to a lot of different people. But for completeness, your definition of success must incorporate its dualistic nature—your success is both being and doing, both active and passive, both inner and outer.

As such, there are *4 Tenets of Success* to consider in your journey of Life Leadership:

#1: Success is self-prescribed.

#2: Success comes through you, not to you.

#3: Success is a habit

#4: Success is a side-effect of your commitment to your Life-Purpose.

Consider *Table 2: Success—Being, Doing, Active, Passive*:

SUCCESS	BEING	DOING
ACTIVE	#1 Success is Self-Prescribed	#3 Success is a Habit
PASSIVE	#2 Success Comes Through You, Not to You	#4 Success is a Side-Effect of Your Commitment to Your Life-Purpose

TABLE 2:   Success—Being, Doing, Active, Passive

WHAT DOES SUCCESS MEAN TO YOU?

The 4 Tenets of Success fit into a model of being/doing/active/passive. Let's now discuss them in turn.

#1: Success is Self-Prescribed (Active Being)

Success, it must be emphasised, should be self-prescribed.

You decide how success is defined. This means being pro-active in knowing who you want to be and what you want to do, then defining and describing all its parameters.

It also means you shouldn't rely on others or society to tell you what they think success for you should be. Most people will only value in you what they value in themselves, which is normally how much money you earn, who you've married, what car you drive, your level of education, your ideal physique, where you live, and what job you have. They'll be more than happy to tell you what they think is right for you and judge you on your ability to live up to their expectations.

In my earlier career as a junior paediatrician, I was outwardly successful. At least in the eyes of what other people expected and deemed as successful. Yet inwardly I was a disaster zone. I was constantly negative to myself and others. I was quick to anger and slow to forgive. I felt stuck in a career I didn't want and sick of a life that wasn't of my choosing. I had followed the path of least resistance, the well-trodden path of school, university (or trade), job, and career. The problem with this typical pathway is that the decisions we make as 18-year-olds determine the path we take throughout our entire life.

Unfortunately, 18-year-olds don't really know what they want to do for the rest of their life. How can they? They're far too young and inexperienced to know. Which is what young adulthood should be about, getting experience. Trying new things. Failing early and learning from your mistakes. Then after a period of years, some necessary life experience has been gained to permit you an educated choice on the path you should follow.

But this rarely happens. What usually happens is that 18-year-olds make decisions on their future based on what others expect of them. They then embark on a career path that might look good on paper but might not be right in the real world. Decades pass, the 18-year-old becomes 28, 38, 48, 58, and at some point begins to wonder if they had made the right decision all those years ago. They have a niggling feeling that something is missing. They yearn to do something they love, not forced to do through economic or social necessity. Most of all, they have a deep craving to become the person they thought they always would—before it's too late.

This sequence of events is common, and it usually results from following someone else's idea of what's best. Your life, though, is so much more than what others define for you, and your personal definition of success is just that, yours. There's a 'U' in success, and that means you. This also means you shouldn't compare yourself to ultra-successful people either. As alluring as it may be, aspiring to a life of the super-rich or super-powerful may turn out to be self-limiting and self-defeating.

Success, as we've said, is a personal brand. It's dependent on your own unique set of circumstances. It's specific to only you. Nobody else knows you like you do. Only you know what success looks like from your point of view. So don't measure your success with someone else's ruler. Be deaf to what others tell you is best, sit down with your thinking hat on, take ownership of who you want to be and what you want to do, and get very clear on how success looks for you.

#2: Success Comes Through You, Not to You (Passive Being)

There are two types of income: active and passive. Active income is where you work for your money. Passive income is where your money works for you. But to get passive income, you need to invest capital. To get 'passive' success, you likewise need to invest time and effort into your Life Purpose and the person you wish to be.

WHAT DOES SUCCESS MEAN TO YOU?

As a Life Leader, you need to invest 100% in your own personal brand of success, and, more importantly, in yourself—mentally, physically, emotionally, spiritually. Financial advisors will tell you to divest your portfolio and don't put all your eggs in one basket. But that's exactly what Life Leaders do: they put all their eggs in one basket and run with it. It really can't happen any other way. It's you we're talking about here, nobody else. It's your success and prosperity we're interested in, not somebody else's.

This means being true to yourself. It means being you in every conceivable situation every second of the day, repeatedly, relentlessly. But first you need to define who you are. You need to stand true to your beliefs in yourself and what you represent, totally. Don't be anything other than you. Don't try to be somebody else. Because success, even greatness, is first built on the foundation of you.

In fact, you—who you really are—is the only foundation on which your personal brand of success can be achieved. It can't be based on anyone else because then it would be their success, not yours, and there's a 'U' in success for a reason. Therefore, make your foundation—your ideal you—a rock on which to build your success.

Your success and prosperity then, as you will experience along your Life Leadership journey, comes through you, not to you. It comes through who you are and what you are being. As the philosopher and writer, James Allen, reminded us:

> *Men do not attract that which they want, but that which they are.*[7]

Therefore look no further than what's inside you—who you are, what you're made of—to find what you're looking for.

That's your power.

---

[7] James Allen, *As a Man Thinketh*, Thomas Y. Crowell Co., 1902

#3: Success is a Habit (Active Doing)

Life Leaders know that success isn't a secret treasure waiting for you to stumble upon and discover its whereabouts. Success is an act of creation.

Any type of winning, any type of achievement, any type of accomplishment, is created through a process—a process of hard work, determination, and unyielding will—which is why it's a habit. No doctor, no scientist, no teacher, no engineer, no lawyer, ever achieved their level of academic success by not studying hours and hours per week, for three, five, even six years and more at university or college. No elite athlete, no footballer, no basketballer, ever made the team by not turning up to practice, by not maintaining a professional level of fitness, by not going the extra mile in pursuit of their goal. No artist, no writer, no dancer, no singer, no musician, ever received critical acclaim by not dedicating themselves to their craft, by not spending tens of thousands of hours painting, writing, dancing, singing, or practicing their instrument.

Dreams don't become real because they are wished into existence. Dreams happen after ten, fifteen, even twenty years of effort. Sometimes more. Just as faith without works is dead, if you have the dream but not the drive, if you have the motive but not the effort, it probably won't happen. Not unless you're extremely lucky, and even then the chances are it won't last very long.

Why? Because the foundations on which your success can be sustained haven't been built. The scientist who discovers the cure for a seemingly 'incurable' disease, the athlete that gets chosen to represent their country at the Olympic Games, the ballerina who lands a position at the Royal Ballet School, know that they haven't achieved success overnight. It's taken years of determination, dedication, and perspiration.

Habit is the Life Leader's go-to process—the habit of right being, right thinking, right action.

#4: Success is a Side-Effect of Your Commitment to Your Life-Purpose (Passive Doing)

Although illness in infancy left her deaf, mute, and blind, Hellen Keller broke through her disabilities and empowered herself to live a rich and fulfilling life. She wrote:

> *Many persons have a wrong idea of what constitutes true happiness. It is not attained through self-gratification but through fidelity to a worthy purpose.*[8]

There is probably no greater motivation than to work for something bigger than yourself. Whether it's fighting for a worthy cause, working for a business you believe in, playing for a sporting team, getting involved in a community project, the important factor is to find something bigger than yourself and commit to it.

Ralph Waldo Emerson, the 19th Century American essayist and lecturer, advised us to hitch our wagon to a star.[9] Like the Big Dipper (which looks like a wagon hitched to a star, doesn't it?) when you think big, plan big, and act big, you'll find favour with the universe.

But whatever cause you align yourself with, whatever purpose you devote yourself to, your first need is commitment and dedication to that cause or purpose. On average, it's estimated that 80% of small businesses fail in the first five years, although it's probably more like 50%.[10] Whatever the true figure is, there's one predominant reason small businesses succeed or fail—*commitment*.

Lack of commitment, or rather lack of *total* commitment, invariably spells failure. Strong, firm, unwavering commitment can be the very thing that turns the odds in favour of success. But

---

[8] Helen Keller, *Helen Keller's Journal 1936–1937*, Doubleday, Doran & Company Inc., Garden City, New York, 1938.

[9] *American Civilization*, essay and lecture, first published in *Atlantic Monthly*, 1862

[10] Longitudinal Business Database, U.S. Census. Five-year survival of the 1977-2000 cohorts of new establishments.

if you're reading this and a thousand and one excuses pop into your head as to why you can't do what you always wanted to do, then I'm sorry to say you're simply not committed. You're not committed to your dreams, and you're not committed to yourself. You don't want it bad enough.

Like my younger 'gunna' self, I wasn't committed to writing the book I always wanted to write. My commitment was lacking because my commitment to myself and my Life Purpose was built on sand and my want was weak. I thought I was a 'doer', but I was only fooling myself. I had a desire to do what I wanted to do but had no commitment because I didn't have the courage to invest my*self* in my dreams and purpose in life. The outcome was neither here nor there. I didn't want it that badly.

Yet, once you make the commitment to the person you were born to be and the path you are meant to follow, you will learn that success and prosperity is a natural outcome or side-effect of that journey.

2 GETTING PAST YOURSELF

THE 3 BARRIERS TO YOUR SUCCESS

THE HUMAN BRAIN has been described as the most complex thing in the universe. Yet, although we understand a great deal about its structure and function, scientists are only scratching the surface to understanding how it fully works.

One model divides the brain into three sections[11] (*Figure 7: The Triune Brain*):

1. Neomammalian (Neocortex – forebrain)
2. Paleomammalian (Limbic – midbrain)
3. Reptilian (Cerebellar – hindbrain)

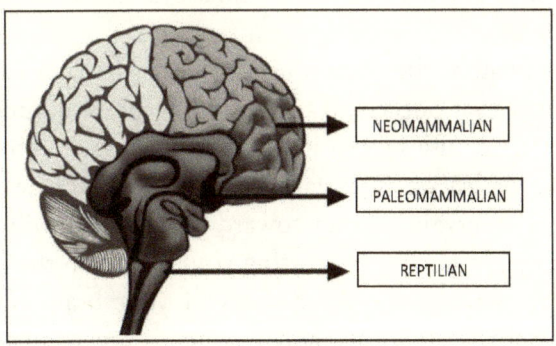

FIGURE 7:   The Triune Brain

Neomammalian means 'new' mammalian. It is the most evolved part of your brain and encompasses the area known as

---

[11] The Triune Theory of the human brain, Paul MacLean.

the neocortex ('new' cortex). This forebrain is responsible for your superior human intelligence, which includes your thought processing, beliefs, reason, self-awareness, analysis, and planning. It is responsible for the conclusions you draw to external stimuli, your perception and your perspective.

Paleomammalian means 'old' mammalian. It developed prior to the neomammalian part of the brain and is therefore less evolved. This midbrain encompasses your emotional processing area of the brain known as the limbic system, which includes the amygdala and hippocampus. Its functions include your imagination, dreams, memory, reward, pleasure and pain. It is responsible for the emotions and feelings you associate with external stimuli.

The reptilian part of the brain is the oldest and therefore least evolved. This hindbrain is situated at the back of your brain at the top of the spinal cord, the area known as the cerebellum. It is responsible for your most basic functions and instincts, including breathing, heartrate, and your involuntary reflexes. It is responsible for the body's sub-conscious reaction to external stimuli.

Unfortunately, the human brain is not wired for success. It's wired for survival. Success, as a general concept, is counterintuitive to the brain because success involves risk taking, and the brain is risk averse. Safety of the organism (you) always comes first. On your Life Leadership journey toward mastery, you will therefore find the biggest barrier preventing your ascent to the next level is *yourself*. Namely, the three parts of your brain responsible for your beliefs, emotions, and instincts—the neomammalian, paleomammalian, and reptilian part of you.

Whatever Life Leadership level you have arrived at, you will need to get past your own internal barriers to get to the next level.

GETTING PAST YOURSELF

INSTINCT BARRIER

The first barrier to overcome on your Life Leadership journey is always your survival instinct. Your reptilian hindbrain is wired to keep you alive at all costs. Along with the amygdala, it is intricately involved with the fight and flight response, which means it will do one of two things when threatened: it will either fight any perceived threat, or it will flee it. Unfortunately, the reptilian brain views any potential change to your circumstances as a threat. Which is why its first instinct is to preserve the status quo and oppose any change.

Your reptilian brain therefore resists any attempt you make to improve yourself, which is counterproductive to your Life Leadership journey. Its concern is that should 'you' change so much you risk becoming unrecognisable to yourself. So whenever your reptilian brain suspects that a change is imminent, it immediately does one of two things—it goes into defence mode, or it goes on the attack.

This makes personal development difficult. By definition, personal development means change, which is threatening to your reptilian ego, and it will either defend or attack your efforts to change in any way.

When in defence (flight) mode, your reptilian brain tries to shield you with justifications and excuses as to why you can't make the changes you want to make. The excuse language is a kind of propaganda to convince you that any change you're considering—thoughts, beliefs, behaviours—aren't necessary. That things are okay just as they are.

Be mindful, then, of any justifying and excuse language you use, which is usually self-depreciating and fault finding.

Here are some examples in the table below:

IT'S UP TO YOU!

JUSTIFYING LANGUAGE	EXCUSE LANGUAGE
'Oh, I'm not very good at that. I always get it wrong.'	'It didn't work out. What could I do?'
'Nobody likes me much.'	'It wasn't my fault.'
'I didn't do very well at school, I'm not very smart.'	'There's just not enough time in the day.'
'That's the way it turned out. I accept my lot. I'm a realist.'	'I knew it would never work, but did they listen to me?'
'Things won't change, so what's the point in trying?'	'Money doesn't grow on trees, you know.'

TABLE 3: Reptilian Brain—Justifying and Excuse Language

In defence mode, the words of justification and excuses are usually words of polar extreme: always, never, can't, won't, ain't, shouldn't, couldn't. When in attack (fight) mode, your reptilian brain uses these same words against other people and circumstances, which is usually the language of 'blame and shame'.

BLAME LANGUAGE	SHAME LANGUAGE
'Why did I listen to you?'	'You never do anything right.'
'It' all your fault!'	'I've got no time for fools.'
'I did what you asked and now look at this mess.'	'You're not very good at this, are you?'
'Why didn't you follow my instructions?'	'That guy's lazy, so don't bother.'
'I knew it'd turn out badly.'	'Why do I put up with this?'

TABLE 4: Reptilian Brain—Blame and Shame Language

It's important to be aware of the language your reptilian brain uses and the feelings it arouses. How you think is how you feel is how you speak; and if you are thinking on the level of your reptilian brain, it can seriously impede your progress along the Life Leadership journey and prevent you from achieving the success and prosperity you want.

EMOTIONAL FEELING BARRIER

The next barrier to overcome is your emotional reactions and feelings. Your paleomammalian midbrain is an emotional hothouse. It is wired to react emotionally to any situation it encounters, and it usually does this through the dual filters of pleasure and pain. If it perceives something as pleasurable, it will react with what we know as positive feelings: happiness, love, excitement, enthusiasm, desire. If it perceives something painful, it will react with what we know as negative feelings: anger, hatred, jealousy, selfishness, bitterness.

Although it's commonplace to interchange the words 'emotions' and 'feelings' to mean the same thing, neuro-researchers make a distinction between them. Emotions are defined as the physical, bodily responses to external stimuli or change. Feelings are the psychological, mental responses to the body's emotions. Think of it as: emotions = body, feelings = mind.

The sequence of stimulus-emotions-feelings goes like this:

Event	Emotion	Feeling
External Stimuli	→ Physical Response	→ Psychological Response

For example, an external threat will evoke a physical emotion such as stress: sweaty palms and brow, fast heartrate, shallow breathing, nausea, the urge to urinate. This in turn evokes a psychological feeling such as fear, dread, anxiety, worry, anger.

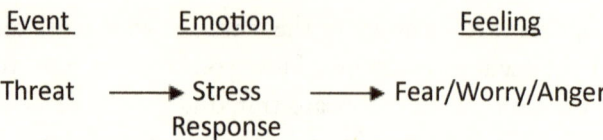

Your physical emotions are genetically programmed responses or reactions that occur in the subcortical midbrain region (e.g. the amygdala). Your psychological feelings, however, are not genetically programmed. Rather, they are psychological programs written by your past experiences, beliefs, thoughts, and memories. They are your associated responses to physical and emotional stimuli.

Your feelings are therefore unique and personal responses to what is happening around you. They are what you have learned to associate with certain external stimuli and physical emotions. They are the cognitive (mental) stories that you have created about your body's emotions.

For instance, your learned associations regarding conflict determines how you feel towards it. Some people avoid conflict at all costs. They associate conflict with certain outcomes they do not like or want, usually pain of some description, physical or psychological. They tell themselves repeatedly, 'I don't like conflict' because their inner cognitive story is 'bad things happen with conflict', which arouses negative feelings. Others have learned to associate conflict with outcomes they do want, such as winning, power, pleasure. They tell themselves repeatedly, 'I look forward to conflict' because their inner cognitive story is 'good things happen with conflict', which arouses positive feelings.

Yet, of all the reactions the paleomammalian brain produces, fear is by far its most powerful. Fear manifests in many guises and there are as many different fears as there are things to fear. Fear of the unknown, fear of death, fear of loneliness, fear of pain, fear of rejection, fear of failure, even fear of success. Medical researchers, however, tell us that we are only born with three fears—the fear of abandonment, the fear of loud noises, and the fear of falling. That's it. Three.

In adults, these three natural fears tend to express themselves as the fear of death, the fear of desertion, and the fear of danger. Which means that of all the fears impacting your life, all but three are learned. Take a moment to look at your biggest fears. The fear of poverty in old age? The fear of illness? The fear of public speaking? The fear of making mistakes? You have learned these fears. Your life experience has taught you to repeatedly express and use these fears to avoid pain. You have created a cognitive story, usually involving a bad ending, associated with an external stimulus, which arouses fear.

The good news is, because all but three fears are learned, they can be unlearned. You can change your story, especially the ending. If you have a fear of needles, that fear can be unlearned. If you have a fear of enclosed spaces, that fear can be unlearned. If you have a fear of spiders, that fear can be unlearned. If you have a fear of failure, that fear can be unlearned.

Fear only has power over you if you let it. Its power is therefore its weakness because its power is determined by your permission to allow it to affect how you behave and to affect your ideas of who you think you are. You are bigger than your fears because you are the creator of them. You therefore have the power to choose against fear and to not let it dictate your thoughts, emotions, and actions.

Because you have this power, you have the power to unlearn all your fears and escape the stranglehold they have on you.[12]

INTELLECT BARRIER

The third barrier to overcome is your intellect.

Your neomammalian forebrain is divided into two hemispheres,

---

[12] We will discuss more about overcoming your fears in the final chapter, *Empower Your Life*.

the left and the right. Your left hemisphere is responsible for your logical and reasoning thought processes. Your right hemisphere is responsible for your creative and artistic thought processes. Both hemispheres are wired to interpret the world through its given lens, and usually one hemisphere predominates, which means you generally view what's happening in the world through the eyes of logic or through the eyes of creativity.

Neither is more correct or important than the other. However, they do share a commonality—beliefs. Both your left and right brain perceive the world through the lens of your belief system. This means you see what you believe.[13]

What stands between you and your true potential, therefore, is the way you think. Denis Waitley, motivational speaker and best-selling author of *The Psychology of Winning*, puts it this way:

> *It's not what you are that holds you back. It's what you think you are not.*[14]

Your belief about yourself—the *way* you think about yourself, *how* you think about yourself, *what* you think about yourself—is a determining factor in your ascent through the levels of Life Leadership. Do you see yourself as successful and prosperous? Or do you see yourself as otherwise? Do you see yourself connected to a higher source of power? Or do you see yourself as disconnected and isolated from everyone and everything?

The flea circus is a great metaphor for how your intellectual brain limits your full potential. Fleas have the incredible ability to leap eighty times their own height. This is the equivalent of a six-foot human jumping four hundred and eighty feet into the air, or

---

[13] We will discus more about beliefs and perception in Chapter 10, *Power Up Your Beliefs*.

[14] Denis Waitley, *Seeds of Greatness: The Ten Best Kept Secrets of Total Success*. New York: Pocket Books, 1983.

over a forty-eight-storey building. However, fleas can be trained to jump only a few inches high.

A flea trainer does this with a simple deception, by placing an upended glass or cup over the fleas. When the fleas try to jump, they hit a ceiling, which is the bottom of the cup. Over time, the fleas learn they can't jump any higher and are tricked into thinking this is the limit of their capabilities. When the cup is removed, the fleas don't return to their normal leaping abilities, rather they are fettered by their training and continue to leap as if the glass or cup was still above them.

Likewise, your brain places a virtual ceiling of thoughts, emotions, and beliefs above you, causing you to live within self-prescribed limitations. It tricks you into believing you're not capable of anything great, that this is as good as it gets. That's your lot, not a single thing more. So you better get used to it and don't try to be anything other than what you are—little, like a flea.

It's easy to fall into this trap, and we all do. When you look at your bank account, what is your response? When you get overlooked for a promotion, what do you feel? When your relationship is rocky, how do you react? When you look yourself in the mirror, what do you think?

Your mind likes to compartmentalise and put things into mental folders and sub-folders. This includes your identity, who you think you are. But when you react to external stimuli such as money in your bank account, your career prospects, your relationship status, your physical appearance, you are sub-consciously labelling and identifying with these things as 'you'. This is how your mind 'belittles' you and makes you flea-like.

But it isn't true. These are just things. They are not you. You are bigger than that. The trick is knowing you're doing it and then telling yourself to stop doing it.

Jay J. Armes lost both hands in an explosion when he was twelve years' old, yet despite his handicap he rose to become one of the

IT'S UP TO YOU!

most successful private investigators of his time. He is cited as saying:

> *You are only handicapped if you think you are. I've spent a lifetime observing people, and I know now, that they set their own limitations, create their own inhibitions. Yet a man can be anything he wants to be, do anything he wants to do, so long as he has a star to steer by.*[15]

Let's consider two characters to illustrate this point of self-limitation. Sally H. is in her thirties. She believes in her abilities and the investment in hard work she has done. She regularly repeats to herself, 'I've worked hard for this. I've devoted myself to this. I deserve this. I'm good enough to succeed!'

David M. is also in his thirties. He is a nice guy that everyone likes, but he has one failing: he sees himself as a perpetual loser. That's his fall-back position in every situation he encounters. Unlike Sally H., the words he regularly repeats to himself are, 'I don't deserve this. I'm not any good at things like this. Other people are better than me.'

On one hand, Sally H. reminds herself that she's capable, she's devoted, she's put in a great amount of effort, she can succeed. She has a vested interest in her personal brand of success. She's committed to it, and part of that commitment is a steadfast belief in who she is—an achiever, a winner. Her thinking is success thinking. Her goal is victory.

On the other hand, David M., although he's a nice fellow and loving family man, doesn't actually think much of himself. It's who he thinks he *isn't* that's holding him back. For whatever has happened in the past to shape his way of thinking, David M. has a vested interest in his personal brand of failure. He's more

---

[15] https://www.policeone.com/investigations/articles/43830-Discouraged-Sometimes-Meet-Private-Investigator-Jay-J-Armes/

committed to mediocrity and non-achievement than he is to success and prosperity. He doesn't believe he's any good. He doesn't think he has the capabilities needed to win. He doesn't believe that his efforts will yield the results he's after. He simply doesn't believe that he is destined for success: winning is for others, not for him.

While Sally H. has nurtured her Life Leadership mindset, David M. has not. David M. is a victim of himself, of his own way of thinking. Unlike Sally H., he has not yet broken through the barrier of his neomammalian brain. Until he does, he will be unable to focus on the ideas and commitment necessary for his success

Below is a table illustrating the difference between how Sally H. and David M. think.

DAVID M.	SALLY H.
'Why me?'	'How can I get things done?'
'I can't do this!'	'I can do this!'
'I'm not very good.'	'I am capable.'
'Even if I try, it won't work.'	'I'll give it a go and make sure it works.'
'Someone else is better suited for this than me.'	'If not me, then who? If not now, then when?'
'I just don't believe it will happen for me.'	'I will make it happen.'

TABLE 5:   David Vs Sally

The difference in their thinking is so massive it's in fact a David and Goliath struggle. Only, in this instance, David loses.

IT'S UP TO YOU!

ASKING THE RIGHT QUESTIONS

The journey through each level of Life Leadership is dependent on your ability to recognise and overcome your natural barriers. As a human being, you have the intrinsic power to transcend your instincts, emotions, and beliefs. For your own benefit, you must use this inner power to transcend yourself.[16]

We mentioned earlier that Life Leaders know their success and prosperity depends on their ability to ask the right questions. Most people, though, ask the wrong kind of questions. When things go wrong, when they don't achieve the outcome or success they were hoping for, they say the one thing that will not help them in any way, shape or form: 'Why me?'

You may have said this to yourself more than once, and it's entirely normal if you did. There is, however, a much better question to ask. One that will give you the answers you're really looking for. Instead of asking, 'Why me?' start to ask, '*How* me?'

'*How* can I improve myself?' '*How* can I make things better?' '*How* can I change and adapt to this situation?' '*How* can I find a solution to this problem?'

Consider the difference in why and how in *Table 6: Asking the Right Questions*. Life Leaders like Sally H. love asking 'How' questions because they get results. They know that:

What you focus on, you experience.

As complex as your brain is, your mind can only focus on seven things at once. Some researchers claim it's even less, only four or five. Yet you are inundated with sensory stimuli every second of the day. Tens of thousands of outside stimuli vie for your attention at any given moment—sights, sounds, smells—but your mind can only handle five, six or seven of these at once,

---

[16] We will discuss more about transcending your limitations in Chapter 13, *Transcend Your Awareness*.

including your thoughts. Which is why it puts up a firewall around what you experience. If it didn't, your mind would seize from the sensory overload.

DAVID M.	SALLY H.
'Why me?'	'How can I get things done?'
'Why can't I get ahead?'	'How can I improve myself?'
'Why does this always happen to me?'	'How can I solve this problem?'
'Why do they always bother me?'	'How can I help?'
'Why does this never work?'	'How can I make things better?'
'Why do I never get what I want?'	'How can I change and adapt?'
'Why is the world always against me?'	'How can I move mountains?'

TABLE 6: Asking the Right Questions

Attention, however, acts like a doorway through the firewall. Your mind only allows those sensory stimuli you focus on to pass through. All else it blocks, which is why you experience what you focus on.

Current research is revealing something interesting about how our beliefs, motivations, emotions, and desires affect how we interpret and perceive the world around us. Research published in *Nature Human Behavior*[17] describes how our motivations and desires, such as our desire for reward, influence our perception in two ways and lead to an inaccurate representation of the world:

---

[17] *Neurocomputational mechanisms underlying motivated seeing*, Yuan Chang Leong et. al., *Nature Human Behaviour*, 2019

1. Perceptual bias: whereby your motivations have a top-down influence on your perceptions; and
2. Response bias: seeing what you wish to see.

You can't always trust your five senses in telling you the full story of what's going on because your perception of reality is often biased, selective, and malleable. Part of the reason are two mental filters that psychologists refer to as our 'Attention Filter' and 'Expectation Filter', which combine to create your own personal firewall.

Your human brain has the processing power of about 120-150 bits per second. When you consider a conversation with someone uses 60 bits per second of processing power, that doesn't leave much more to process everything else that's happening. Practically, this means that your short-term memory is only able to store five to seven pieces of information at any one time (where these 'chunks' of information don't exceed 120 bits per second).[18] Some researchers have even said it's even lower, at only four pieces of information at any one time.

This is where your attention filter steps in. Millions of neurones collectively combine to create your attention filter, which sifts out unnecessary information, the stuff you really don't need to know. Most information is dealt with by your sub-conscious, leaving your attention filter to let through what's important to know on the conscious level. In fact, your attention filter is one of your most important mental resources because it determines which aspects of the inner and outer world you need to deal with at any particular moment.

Think of a time when you have driven for a long while and arrived at your destination with little recall of the outside scenery you passed along the way. This perceptual bias is your attention

---

[18] George Miller, *The Magical Number 7, Plus or Minus Two: Some Limits on Our Capacity for Processing Information*, Psychological Review, 1956

filter at work. It works like a sieve to disregard anything you are currently not focused on.

Your expectation filter, on the other hand, works like a mirror, letting you see what you expect to see and hear what you want to hear. For instance, if you took a trip to Scotland hoping to see the Loch Ness Monster, you might catch a glimpse of something in the far distant waves of the loch and interpret it as the shape of the monster you wanted to see. This response bias is how your mind turns shadows and flashes of light into sightings of things that aren't there.

But this trick of the mind is also a big problem in science. Scientists know that the simple act of observing an experiment can affect the outcome of that experiment, which is known as 'observer influence'. Many researchers have been caught out because they have observed exactly what they wanted or expected to observe. Double-blind experiments are used to try and counteract this phenomenon and minimise the impact of the observing scientist on the outcome.

Our perceptual and response biases are in play every day. Expectant mothers, for instance, see babies in prams everywhere they go. It's called the 'new baby syndrome'. They haven't magically conjured babies into their world, only that their focus is now centred on the arrival of their newborn child. They've trained their brain to allow the perception of babies in prams to get through their mental firewall. The number of babies they encounter in their day-to-day world hasn't changed, only their experience of them. They see what they want to see.

Likewise, if you're considering buying a new car. If you have a particular model and colour in mind, such as a silver Mercedes, your mind is now focused on experiencing that and you start seeing more silver Mercedes cars on the roads.

These same psycho-mechanics are at play when you ask 'Why me?' questions. When your attention is focused on the answers to the reasons 'why', you will invariably find those answers. But these answers won't help you find a solution to your problems.

Asking, 'How can I?' trains your brain to focus on solutions that show you how you can. You start to see solutions that were otherwise blocked from your awareness because your attention wasn't previously focused on them. Like babies in prams and silver Mercedes cars, the solutions are always there.

You just need to ask the right questions.

THE PRESCRIPTION FOR YOUR BEST LIFE

Everyone has two states or conditions: the place where they are now (current), and the place where they want to be (desired). For many, getting to their desired place is difficult for several reasons. Money, resources, motivation, time, but generally it's the lack of knowhow. It's not their fault, it's just that their education system hasn't taught them how to become the person they were meant to be or to find their niche in life.

One of the best questions to therefore ask is this: 'How can I be who I want to be and do what I want to do?'

That translates to: how can you get into Life Quadrant #1, the desired quadrant, in The Empowered Living Index?

The answer is captured in *Figure 8: The Empowered Living Index—Reconnect, Realign, Rejuvenate.*

If you recognise that your current quadrant is Life Quadrant #4, you will feel a disconnection between your outward success and your inner success. Your finances and career may well be on track, but you have become detached from who you really are and the person you want to be. This manifests as the feeling that you have become a person unrecognisable to who you hoped you would be, that the 'real' you is buried and trapped beneath layers of false personality. When you look in the mirror, you don't recognise who you are anymore.

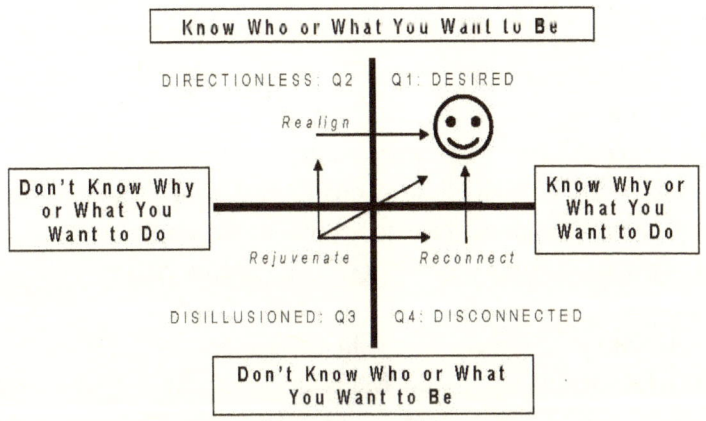

FIGURE 8: The Empowered Living Index—
Realign, Reconnect, Rejuvenate

In this quadrant you work to live; you are doing well but not being well. To move into the desired quadrant, a *reconnection* with your Ideal Persona is required. Your focus will be on implementing the first of the 3 Golden Rules: *Rule #1: Define Who You Are*.

If you recognise that your current quadrant is Life Quadrant #2, you may feel you are on track to becoming the person you want to be, but you are disorientated on your outward path. You are not doing what you want to do, and you're not where you want to be right now. This is the feeling of searching for something you know is missing but not quite knowing what that 'something' is.

In this quadrant you yearn to find your niche, that place where you truly belong, the place where you can finally express the person you are. To move into the desired quadrant, a *realignment* with your values and Life Purpose is required. Your focus will be on implementing the second of the 3 Golden Rules: *Rule #2: Determine What You Want*.

If you recognise that your current quadrant is Life Quadrant #3, you will feel disillusioned with a lot of what's happening. You have not become the person you thought you would, you are not doing what you want to do, you are not where you want to be. You have lost much of the passion and enthusiasm for life.

In this quadrant you feel that your endeavours go unrewarded and that nothing you do is worth the time or effort. You despair that nothing will ever change for the better, that this is as good as it gets. To move into the desired quadrant, a *rejuvenation* of your Inner Power is required. Your focus will be on implementing the third of the 3 Golden Rules: *Rule #3: Design How to Achieve It*.

But before you do, because you are starting from a low base, you will first need to focus on the first two rules, Define Who You Are and Determine What You Want. Once you have implemented these rules, you will have laid the foundations to implement the third rule.

Whatever your circumstances are right now, these 3 Golden Rules are what I call the prescription for your best life. They prescribe the process to get to Life Quadrant #1, Life Leadership mastery. These rules focus your thoughts on 'how you can' achieve who you want to be and what you want to do, and away from 'why you haven't' previously been able to. They train your brain to focus toward the future ('how me?') and decouple it from the caboose of the past ('why me?').

Because what you focus on, you experience.

3 THE LIFE LEADERSHIP STRATEGY

GETTING TO MASTERY

IN ANY GAME, strategies improve your chances of winning. The Game of Life is no different. Life Leaders follow a strategy to circumvent their barriers and achieve success, and this is normally a process of how to *visualise*, *plan*, and *manifest* success:

-> Visualise Your Ideal: who are you going to be, what do you want to do, and why?

-> Plan Your Journey: what needs to be done and how are you going to do it?

-> Manifest Your Reality: what action is required and who will execute the plan?

There are 4 Life Leadership Skills to facilitate your strategy:

- ♦ Life Skill #1–Who
- ♦ Life Skill #2–Why
- ♦ Life Skill #3–What
- ♦ Life Skill #4–How

These Life Leadership Skills help you answer the big questions:

1. Who are you?
2. Why are you here?
3. What do you do?
4. How do you do it?

Each diamond level is designed to attain a competent skillset

IT'S UP TO YOU!

before you can graduate to the next level. Ideally, it should take about two years to get to Life Leadership mastery, the level of black diamond. It can be done quicker, but don't short-change yourself. Like rungs on a ladder, the levels of the Life Leadership model are meant to be ascended one at a time in order. You're only doing yourself a disservice if you don't.

Cutting corners is also not advised. You don't want to ascend so fast that you don't have the skillset supporting you—your next level is only as strong as the base beneath it. If you haven't spent time building your skills at each level, you will crash all the way to the bottom at the first sign of trouble. Then you'll have to start all over again and rebuild.

You don't want to be too slow either. Taking ten years to ascend to black diamond mastery will sap your motivation and risk the return of old habits, habits that sabotaged your success in the very beginning. Momentum through the levels is the best approach. Don't get too stuck and let things slide.

As Bruce Lee advised, there are only plateaus in life and you must not stay there, you must go beyond them. If you work with consistency on the practices and challenges you face, you will eventually get to Life Leadership mastery.

LIFE LEADERSHIP PRACTICES

Ascending the diamond levels is done by completing the required practice at your current level. These are determined by the three axis points in The Golden Triangle, and there are 9 Life Leadership Practices to complete the Life Leadership program at purple diamond level, which will be discussed in the following chapters.

In the Life Leadership Model, the nine diamond levels are divided into three tiers:

THE LIFE LEADERSHIP STRATEGY

Tier #1: Focus—Orange, Brown, Yellow
Tier #2: Success—Blue, Red, Black
Tier #3: Elite—Green, White, Purple

Each tier represents a different level of understanding. For instance, your depth of knowledge will be greater in Tier #3: Elite than in Tier #2: Success, which in turn is greater than your understanding in Tier #1: Focus. Think of Tier #1: Focus as basic, student knowledge, Tier #2: Success as more competent, teacher level knowledge, and Tier #3: Elite as mastery level knowledge.

The aim of this book is to get you to black diamond at the top of Tier #2: Success, but we will also discuss the levels within Tier #3: Elite should you wish to complete your Life Leadership journey.

TIER	LIFE LEADERSHIP JOURNEY	LIFE LEADERSHIP ATTAINMENT				LIFE LEADERSHIP MASTERY	LIFE LEADERSHIP PRACTICE
ELITE #3	PURPLE DIAMOND	✓✓	✓✓	✓✓	✓✓	✓✓	EMPOWER
	WHITE DIAMOND	✓✓	✓✓	✓✓	✓✓	✓✓	ABUNDANCE
		✓	✓	✓	✓	✓	
	GREEN DIAMOND	✓✓	✓✓	✓✓	✓✓	✓✓	BEING
SUCCESS #2	BLACK DIAMOND	✓	✓	✓	✓	✓	TRANSCEND
	RED DIAMOND	✓	✓	✓	✓	✗	VISION
	BLUE DIAMOND	✓	✓	✓	✗	✗	VALUES
FOCUS #1	YELLOW DIAMOND	✓	✓	✗	✗	✗	BELIEF
	BROWN DIAMOND	✓	✗	✗	✗	✗	NICHE
	ORANGE DIAMOND	✗	✗	✗	✗	✗	CHARACTER

TABLE 9: The Life Leadership Model—3 Tiers

IT'S UP TO YOU!

Each tier has three Life Practices. In the below example, Tier #1 understanding of your 'I Am' is focused on the Life Practice: Building Your Character. As you ascend to Tier #2, blue diamond level, your understanding of your 'I Am' is focused on the Life Practice: Refine Your Values. At Tier #3, green diamond level, your understanding of your 'I Am' is focused on the Life Practice: Your Natural State of Being.

AXIS	TIER #1: FOCUS	TIER #2: SUCCESS	TIER #3: ELITE
I AM (*Being*)	#1 Build Your Character	#4 Refine Your Values	#7 Your Natural State of Being
I WILL (*Intent*)	#2 Find Your Niche	#5 Retain Your Vision	#8 Attitudes of Abundant Living
I CAN (*Power*)	#3 Power Up Your Beliefs	#6 Transcend Your Awareness	#9 Empower Your Life

TABLE 10: 3 Tiers—Life Leadership Practices

The axis points—I Am, I Will, I Can—don't change through your Life Leadership journey, only the *depth* of your understanding of them. Which is what each Life Practice is designed to help you achieve. Each follow the rules as set out by The Diamond Triangle—Define, Determine, Design—to master the essential factors in your success and prosperity: being, intent, power, and purpose.

That way, nothing gets missed on your ascent through the levels of Life Leadership.

LIFE LEADERSHIP ENCAPSULATED

In the Life Leadership Model, each Life Practice is specific for your current diamond level. For example, your journey will usually begin at orange diamond level, which requires you to follow Rule #1: Define Who You Are and its axis position 'I Am'. At Tier #1:

THE LIFE LEADERSHIP STRATEGY

Focus, the Life Practice to complete is 'Build Your Character'. Successful completion of the Life Practice accomplishes your Life Skill at this level, 'Who'.

We will discuss the 9 Life Leadership Practices of each diamond level in later chapters. In the meantime, *Table 11: Life Leadership Encapsulated* summarises all the levels, rules, axes, practices, and skills, and how they fit within the three tiers of the Life Leadership model. You will also see that Life Skill #2–Why is a special skill because it is the common thread linking all 9 Life Leadership Practices.

DIAMOND LEVEL	LIFE AXIS	LIFE RULE	LIFE TIER	LIFE PRACTICE	LIFE SKILL
ORANGE		#1 DEFINE WHO YOU ARE	#1	#1 CHARACTER	#1 WHO
BLUE	I AM (BEING)		#2	#4 VALUES	#2 WHY
GREEN		#2 DETERMINE WHAT YOU WANT	#3	#7 BEING	#3 WHAT
BROWN		#2 DETERMINE WHAT YOU WANT	#1	#2 NICHE	#2 WHY
RED	I WILL (INTENT)		#2	#5 VISION	#3 WHAT
WHITE		#3 DESIGN HOW TO ACHIEVE IT	#3	#8 ABUNDANCE	#4 HOW
YELLOW		#3 DESIGN HOW TO ACHIEVE IT	#1	#3 BELIEFS	#4 HOW
BLACK	I CAN (POWER)		#2	#6 TRANSCEND	#2 WHY
PURPLE		#1 DEFINE WHO YOU ARE	#3	#9 EMPOWER	#1 WHO

TABLE 11: Life Leadership Encapsulated

IT'S UP TO YOU!

You can see that the Life Skills are the building blocks of your Life Axes, which is why they are so important. For instance:

-> I Am (axis of *being*) is built with Life Skills Who, Why, What:

- Who are you?
- Why are you here?
- What is the substance of your being?

-> I Will (axis of *intent*) is built with Life Skills Why, What, How:

- Why do you want to achieve your intentions?
- What do you need to do to achieve your intentions?
- How are you going to achieve your intentions?

-> I Can (axis of *power*) is built with Life Skills How, Why, Who:

- How will you empower yourself?
- Why will you empower yourself?
- Who is the source of your power?

This diagram illustrates how your Life Leadership Skills fit into The Diamond Triangle.

We will now discuss each Life Leadership Skill in turn and its essential role in the success you want to achieve.

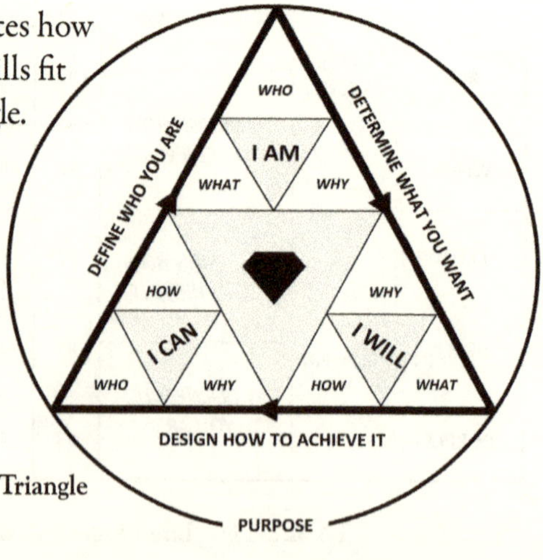

FIGURE 9: The Diamond Triangle —Life Leadership Skills

PART 2

LIFE LEADERSHIP
SKILLS

4 LIFE SKILL #1: WHO

WHO DO YOU THINK YOU ARE?

Who are you?

Do you know the answer to that question? Life Leaders know it's the first step in becoming successful. Which is why they first apply themselves to Life Skill #1–Who.

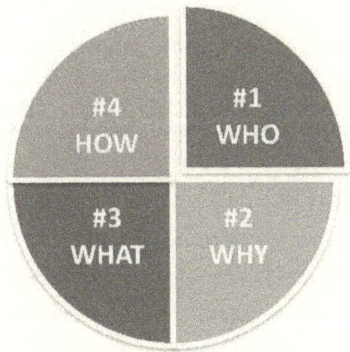

FIGURE 10:   Life Skill #1–Who

If you had asked some of the greatest people in history who they were—Winston Churchill, Mahatma Gandhi, Mother Teresa, Nelson Mandela, Jesus—they would've answered in a flash. They had come to know without a doubt who and what they were. It was their identity, their motivation, their reason for being.

The statement 'I am' is one of the most powerful phrases in the human language. Great and successful people realise this. They know that a deep-seated knowing of who they are, of knowing *instantly*, focuses Life's power in the same way a magnifying lens focuses the power of sunlight. With a simple magnifying glass, you hold in your hand the power to burn down a forest. Imagine what you could do with the power of 'I am'.

This power is open to everyone. However, few use it consciously. Life Leaders, though, deliberately maximise the power of knowing who they are to fuel their success. Others—the moderately successful—only have a vague idea of who they are, and so only attain a moderate level of success. Others still—the least successful—have no idea of who they are, nor that their success comes through them, and their level of success is a daily reflection of that knowing.

Take a moment to reflect on the level of success you've reached to now. Are you highly successful, moderately successful, or not at all successful? Are you happy with the level of your success? Is there something holding you back?

The 80:20 rule applies in this instance: 20% of factors limiting your success are outside your control, and 80% of limiting factors are within you. But this is good news. You can control 80% of the factors implicit in your success. No matter where you're at or what you've achieved, no matter your age, sex or race, you hold the key to your future prosperity. Nobody else. Not even your circumstances, because life-circumstances don't make or break who you are, they *reveal* who you are.

You are in possession of everything you need to succeed. That key is the power to choose; and the most potent use of this key is the power to choose who you are, because this determines everything. Victor Frankl, holocaust survivor and author of *Man's Search for Meaning*,[19] discovered through surviving two Nazi death camps that no matter what happens to you, no matter what fate befalls

---

[19] Victor Frankl. *Man's Search for Meaning*, Beacon Press, 1959 (first published 1946, Austria)

LIFE SKILL #1: WHO

you, you always have the power to choose—you always have free will:

> *Everything can be taken from a man but one thing: the last of the human freedoms—to choose one's attitude in any given set of circumstances, to choose one's own way.*

He is also attributed as saying:

> *Between stimulus and response there is a space. In that space is our power to choose our response. In our response lies our growth and our freedom.*

In that space between stimulus and response is *you*. You reside in that space between what's happening outside you and your reaction to what's happening inside, between action and reaction. Your neomammalian forebrain doesn't live in that space, nor does your paleomammalian or reptilian brain. They live in the world of thoughts, emotions, and instincts.

But that is not who you are.

YOU ARE NOT YOUR THOUGHTS

Psychologists estimate we have between 12,000 and 60,000 thoughts a day. Although some argue it's far less, some argue it's in fact far more. What isn't contentious is that we do have thousands of thoughts flowing through our minds every day.

René Descartes, the 17th Century French philosopher, famously wrote, Cogito ergo sum: *I think, therefore I am.*[20]

He was pointing to the thinker behind your thoughts, your

---

[20] *'Je pense, donc je suis.'* René Descartes, *Discours de la méthode pur bien conduire a raison, et chercher la vérité dans les sciences* (*Discourse on the Method of Rightly Conducting One's Reason and of Seeking Truth in the Sciences*), 1637

conscious awareness, not the products of that consciousness—your thoughts, your beliefs, your emotions, your instincts. Descartes insists that you are not these products. You are the creator of those thoughts. You are the power that can choose who you are.

Just as you are not your thoughts, neither are you your emotions or desires. Emotions are just states of being. They are not 'you' per se, just a state of existence in which you have immersed yourself. Think of emotions and feelings as bath water. When you immerse yourself in the bath, you might say the water is hot, warm or cold. But you don't say the water temperature is you. It's just an experience. Likewise, anger, happiness, frustrations, fear, and all your other emotions and feelings are just an experience, a state of being you are immersed in. They are not you. Like your thoughts, you have created them.

So too you are not your body. Your body is in a perpetual cycle of birth and rebirth. Doctors estimate that over an average lifetime of 75 years, the human body is replaced at least seven times, and it could be even more. That means every single cell in your body, and it's happening fast. The body you have now—it's bones, muscles, skin, stomach, liver, blood, brain, lungs, heart—will not be the same body by the time you finish this book and put it down. This means you're not the same 'you' you were yesterday, or even an hour ago.

So, if you're not your thoughts, your emotions, or your body, who are you?.

TAKING OWNERSHIP

The truth is, you define who you are.

You actually do it all the time. Unfortunately, it probably happens on autopilot, with little thought or consideration. Life Leaders, however, do it consciously, with great thought and consideration. They are in full control of the process of defining who they are and acknowledge the responsibility for it, but they also know that responsibility stems from taking ownership. If you don't own something, you have little responsibility for it, if any. Taking ownership of who you are is therefore a prerequisite for taking responsibility for who you are.

So your first step on your Life Leadership journey is to own who you are, define who you are, and take responsibility for who you are. If you are reluctant to do this, society or somebody else will gladly do it for you. They will gladly mould you in the image of who and what they want for themselves, invariably for their own benefit.

Eleanor Roosevelt, the First Lady of the United States from 1933-1945, said:

> *When you adopt the standards and values of someone else or a community or a pressure group, you surrender your own integrity. You become, to the extent of your surrender, less of a human being.* [21]

Life Leaders don't let others tell them who they are. So don't allow yourself to be moulded in the image of others. Certainly learn from others, but don't accept their definition of you.

Don't surrender your integrity and become less of a human being.

THE POWER OF I AM

Because your personal brand of success begins with who you are, your vision of yourself is the starting point of your success. It really is the most important part of the process. Get it right and everything else that follows will fall into place. So make that vision

---

[21] Eleanor Roosevelt, *You Learn by Living: Eleven Keys for a More Fulfilling Life*, Westminster John Knox Press, 1960 (revised edition).

a healthy vision. It doesn't matter what age you are right now; what matters is that you actively seek to put into place the truest vision of *who you want to be* so that your future success can be grown from solid roots.

This entails self-nurture. When my wife is in the garden and notices a plant that isn't doing so well, she doesn't blame the plant for not flowering or bearing fruit. Rather, she seeks the cause of the malnutrition, the reason for why the plant isn't getting what it needs to thrive. Invariably, the problem is in the soil and environment in which the plant is growing, not the plant itself. The soil's dryness and lack of minerals, competing weeds, and available sunlight need attending to if the plant is to eventually flower and bear fruit.

So too you must seek the reason for why you are not maximising your full potential. The problem is not with who you are. Your potential is unlimited. The problem is invariably the internal environment in which you inhabit—your mindset—over which you have a great deal of control. Your 'I Am' cannot grow if your mind is a desert, or it isn't fed the right nutrients. It cannot develop sufficiently if it has to compete with a jungle of mental weeds, or it is trapped in shady thoughts.

But as the first axis of your success and prosperity, your 'I Am' is the acorn from which the mighty oak grows. Plant it in a fertile mind, nurture it with intentional thoughts, ideas and images, and who you are will grow into something bigger and better than you could have ever dreamed.

5 LIFE SKILL #2: WHY

THE HAPPINESS FORMULA

DEFINING YOUR 'I AM' is the very first thing you do on your Life Leadership journey. Accomplishing Life Skill #1–Who, is the foundational stone of your 'I Am' axis and is the primary focus of orange diamond level. It is also the final building block of your 'I Can' axis, which is the focus of purple diamond level. Life Skill #1–Who is therefore your alpha and omega, the first and last thing you do on your Life Leadership journey.

Life Skill #2–Why is the second building block in your 'I Am' axis, and the primary focus of brown diamond level. It is also the first building block in your 'I Will' axis at blue diamond level and the second building block of your 'I Can' axis at black diamond level (see *Figure 9: The Diamond Triangle—Life Leadership Skills*).

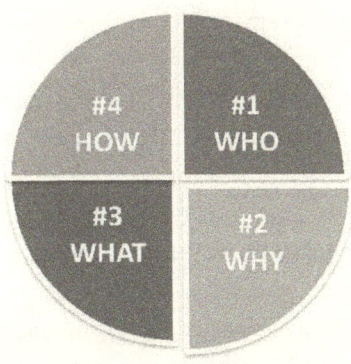

FIGURE 11:   Life Skill #2–Why

Life Skill #2–Why is your linking skill because it links the 'why' of who you are with the 'why' of what you do and the 'why' of how you do it—it links the reason of your being with the reason of your doing. Your 'Why' is your purpose, and this has very powerful consequences because studies have shown that ascribing meaning and purpose significantly affects your happiness and wellbeing.

In fact, there's even a scientific formula for happiness and wellbeing. Positive psychologists have discovered three key elements to happiness and put them into a formula:[22]

$$H = S + C + V$$

- -> **H** is your enduring level of happiness (as opposed to fleeting moments of happiness).
- -> **S** is your set range (genetic variable).
- -> **C** is your circumstances or conditions of your life (environmental variable).
- -> **V** represents actions under your voluntary control (psychological variable).

This isn't meant to be a mathematical formula, rather a guide to how you can improve your wellbeing. Not every element has equal influence over your happiness, however. For instance, 50% of your happiness is determined by your set range, 40% by your voluntary actions and choices, and only 10% by your circumstances or conditions in which you live.

This is why fame and fortune can't buy you happiness. Your circumstances can only ever make up 10% of your total emotional wellbeing. Some external things do make a difference and influence your happiness, such as marriage, religion, and living in a tolerant society. But to be consistently happier, you are better off focusing

---

[22] Martin Seligman, *Authentic Happiness: Using the New Positive Psychology to Realize Your Potential for Lasting Fulfillment*, Atria Books, 2004

LIFE SKILL #2: WHY

less on external, material things, which can be expensive, temporary and impractical, and more on the things that have greater impact, like the choices and decisions you make. The question you need to answer is:

> *Has your efforts to improve your living conditions to date affected your happiness and wellbeing in any significant way?*

Your set range is your biological comfort zone, the level to which you naturally gravitate. Think of your set range as an apartment block. Some people live on the ground floor, others halfway up, and others in the penthouse at the top. Those who have a higher set range are happier on average than those with a lower set range. The people in the penthouse are happier than those on the ground floor.

Your set range, however, is controlled to a large degree by your genetics, which you can't do much about, and is pretty much a fixed variable. Some people are born in the penthouse and are naturally happier than others. That's just the way it is, but it's not all doom and gloom if your set range is in the ground floor. Your happiness isn't set in stone. It can be readjusted.

This is where your voluntary actions and choices are important. Because you can affect this part of the happiness equation the most, it will have the greatest impact on your overall state of being. The best thing you can do for your happiness and wellbeing, therefore, is to choose meaning. When you ascribe positive meaning and purpose to the things that have happened, are happening, or will happen, you skew the happiness equation in your favour. Because when you find purpose, you make meaningful choices. When you make meaningful choices, you take meaningful action. When you take meaningful action, you achieve intended results. Results that are intentional make you happy and fulfilled.

Another technique is to take the virtual elevator up to the penthouse. You 'feel' your way to the top by regularly focusing on the happiness you want to experience more of. This you do through finding your 'happy place', the moments in the past where you felt most happiness. You then bring that happy moment or moments into your present through visualisation, meditation or contemplation. If you do this regularly (several times a day), you will begin to readjust your overall sense of wellbeing to a higher level than what you are currently used to experiencing. Your happiness will be upwardly mobile.

This is self-empowering. Your actions and choices alone can affect your happiness more than your genetic set range and your life circumstances.

Your happiness is in your control.

MEANING AND PURPOSE

Meaning not only has an effect on your emotional wellbeing on a short-term basis, but also long-term. Ascribing meaning to your life has a positive effect throughout the entire course of your life.

For instance, meaning and purpose improves your self-belief and self-esteem. This in turn builds your self-confidence. You feel you can successfully meet challenges and overcome obstacles. You feel capable of achieving your goals. You feel a sense of competence and accomplishment. You feel successful.

Meaning and purpose also breeds optimism and hope. You believe that life will change for the better, that circumstances will not necessarily stay the same or get worse. You start seeing solutions to problems that you were previously blind to. You start seeking help to improve yourself and others. You stop saying, 'Why me?' and start asking 'How can I?'

Meaning and purpose also channels your focus and concentration. You get into the 'flow' quicker and easier, which

LIFE SKILL #2: WHY

is a powerful source of wellbeing. Flow is the term coined by psychologist Mihaly Czikszentmihalyi and is the state of intense absorption where you forget yourself and your surroundings, especially when you are doing something creative:

> *The best moments in our lives are not the passive, receptive, relaxing times... The best moments usually occur when a person's body or mind is stretched to its limits in a voluntary effort to accomplish something difficult and worthwhile.*[23]

It is meaning and purpose that extract the best moments in your life. This taps into a fundamental truth that Life Leaders know very well and, unfortunately, many dismiss or ignore. Not only do you define who you are, but also:

You determine the meaning of your life.

Not anyone else. Not your mother, your father, your partner, your boss, your best friend. Only you. Because that's the nature of free will—you have the power of self-determination.

So what meaning do you ascribe to your life?

Why do you do what you do? Why were you born? Does your life have purpose?

When Michael Schumacher was being interviewed at the end of his Formula 1 career, he told the reporter, 'I was born to race motorcars.' He believed with every fibre in his body that racing was his life purpose. He didn't question it; he just knew that racing was what he had to do. He was a born racer, and he did everything in his power to fulfil his purpose.

I remember that interview vividly. When he looked into the

---

[23] Mihaly Czikszentmihalyi, *Flow: The Classic Work on how to Achieve Happiness*, Random House, 2002

camera, it was as though he was speaking directly through the TV to me. I remember thinking I knew exactly how he felt because I had always known I was born to write books. I was a born writer, a messenger.

My advice, therefore, is to think very seriously about your life purpose. To think what it is you were born to be. Meaning and purpose is your lifeblood. Not only does it affect your happiness and wellbeing, it is imperative to your human identity. As Carl Jung, the founder of analytical psychology, said:

Man cannot stand a meaningless life.

Some psychologists go further and say that meaning is a distinctive human trait. Meaning is being, in other words, even at your cellular level. Yet, although today we have greater means to live, we are at risk of losing what it means to live. There are a great many who say there is no meaning to life. You're born, you spend some time here on earth, then you die. That's it. Pointless. There is no 'Why?' because we all die. Everything is futile. Death defeats life, and nihilism defeats meaning, every single time.

I understand this concern, yet paradoxically, this nihilistic belief ascribes meaning by not ascribing meaning: the meaning of life is that it has no meaning. This is important because the meaning you ascribe to your life is akin to your personal brand of success. First, you must define it yourself lest somebody else defines it for you. Second, you must own it—you must take ownership of your meaning and you must be committed to it.

If you fail to do these two things, your meaning is not your own; it'll be somebody else's. Consequently, your life will lack integrity, it will lack worth, and it will also lack value. On the flipside, a life brimming with meaning and purpose is a life brimming with value and worth. To give meaning to your life, therefore, is to value who you are, what you do, and where you're going.

LIFE SKILL #2: WHY

And how much you value who you are adds meaning to who you are.

WHY YOU NEED A WHY?

When you take a bus, train, plane, car, or any other means of transport, you invariably know where you want to go. You know your destination before you embark on your journey. But how many people go through life not knowing the destination they're heading to? You wouldn't spend 70-80 minutes sitting on a bus not knowing where the bus is taking you, so why would you spend 70-80 years travelling through life not knowing where you are going?

Steve L. is a married father with a young family. He graduated from university five years ago but is not working in the field in which he studied. He claims there are no jobs for what he wants to do, so really what's the point in trying? When pressed to explain what he actually does want to do, he says, 'I don't know.' When asked why he studied that particular degree, he says, 'I thought it'd be good. It's better to have a degree than not have one.' He also can't tell you where he sees himself, or where he would like to be, in five years' time.

Vickie T., on the other hand, never went to university and probably dropped out of high school. She married young, had kids in her late teens and early twenties, worked multiple jobs in retail and hospitality, then divorced her husband soon after the birth of her third child. But something happened around the time she turned thirty. She found a cause to which she fully committed herself and it changed her life.

She discovered a passion for helping autistic kids to read and write and to understand and cope with their emotions, which, as any parent of autistic children will tell you, is extremely difficult and challenging. She has even written a series of books to help autistic children and their parents, and she has created online courses and workshops based on those books. Her energy and vitality seem endless.

Where Steve L. appears lost and lacks ambition, Vickie T. is focussed and driven to succeed. In fact, her focus is so laser sharp it seems to cut through any obstacle or challenge. But why is Steve floundering and Vickie flourishing? Why can't Steve see the woods from the trees, whereas Vickie makes her own path through the forest?

Vision.

Vickie has it and Steve doesn't. Life Leaders like Vickie have a clear direction as to where they want to go and who they want to be. They might not yet have arrived at their destination, but they know where they're going. In fact, they have arrived at their destination in their *mind* before they have arrived physically.

As Arnold Schwarzenegger once told an interviewer:

> *Create a vision of who you want to be, and then live into that picture as if it were already there.*

When Michelangelo created the statue of David, he didn't see the block of marble. He saw David already inside the marble and then set about chipping away the marble until David emerged from it. Michelangelo 'saw' what was already there. He could visualise the end result, and then went to work on manifesting that vision and making it real.

But this is the vital point:

> *Successful people know what they want and where they're going.*

They are very specific. They are not lost. Madness still happens around them. Difficulties still arise. Yet even in the stress and challenges of everyday living, they have orientated themselves in the direction they want to go. They know who they are and where they want to arrive at. They also know how they want to get there and when they want to be there. Their vision lifts the fog of uncertainty, giving them a clear sight ahead.

They have clarity. They have developed the long-sighted, 20/20 vision of Life Leadership and can see beyond the horizon.

Below is a comparison of meaningless and purposeful vision:

MEANINGLESS	PURPOSEFUL
Joyless and noncommittal	Passionate and committed
Vague and directionless	Focussed and unidirectional
Defeatist and procrastinating	Resilient and enduring
Anxious and stressed	Mindful and composed
Pessimistic and doubtful	Optimistic and hopeful
Uncertain and desponding	Self-Belief and confidence
Indifferent and uncaring	Enthusiastic and driven

TABLE 12: Meaningless Vs Purposeful Vision

Vision and purpose empower Vickie to strive forward, to move in the direction she knows is the right path for her. The lack of vision disempowers Steve. He feels incapable of moving his life forward, seemingly going around and around in circles. For here is the truth of Steve's situation to take heed:

A lack of purpose makes you blind to your own inner power.

Disappointments and failures visit both Steve and Vickie. But whereas Steve gets bogged down in the futility of life and gives up easily, Vickie keeps moving forward, one step at a time, in the direction of her vision. Purpose makes her suffering bearable, and gives her resilience and durability. The lack of purpose makes Steve's suffering unbearable, and he becomes defeatist and pessimistic.

This is backed up by research.[24] People without purpose are vulnerable to anxiety, depression, substance abuse, and boredom. People with life purpose, however, fare better. They have better health outcomes. They sleep better, they have healthier behaviours, they have a lower risk of heart problems, and they have better functioning and independence with ageing. What's more, they also have a 20% lower risk of death.

Like your success and prosperity, these health benefits are a side-effect of your dedication to your life purpose. They are an unintended measure of success in themselves.

If only for that, that's why you need a Why.

THE EVOLUTION OF YOU

Purpose and meaning are integral to your evolution as a Life Leader, and therefore your success and prosperity. Evolution, for our purposes, is your growth into a more sophisticated and enlightened person, the transcendence to a more successful you. Survival alone is not a driver for personal evolution. If your life is only about surviving, if it's only about getting through to the next sunrise, any personal growth or success will not happen in any significant way.

In truth, the reverse will probably result, a decline of personal habits and the eventual descent to animal-like behaviour. I call this survival-at-any-cost mentality the 'junkyard dog' mentality, just scrapping over any morsel to live. But there is more to your life than just surviving and snatching at anything you can get.

Something else is needed to propel your evolution forward.

---

[24] Mount Sinai Medical Center. *Have a sense of purpose in life? It may protect your heart.* ScienceDaily, 2015

LIFE SKILL #2: WHY

Something else is needed to drive you toward a more successful you. Simple survival just won't do it. Survival just begets more of itself, nothing else, a Groundhog Day existence that repeats itself over and over until the end of your days. But purpose and meaning will do it.

When the 'need' for survival is superseded by a 'reason' to survive, purpose and meaning are born. When you find your reason to survive, you find your reason to live. You find the reason you were born. You find the meaning of your life.

You find purpose, at every level of your existence.

YOUR FRAME OF REFERENCE

Your Why? is also your frame of reference.

A ship is built around its ribs and frame. Without which, its exterior cladding is flimsy and unseaworthy. Likewise, people need a strong and stable frame on which to build their identity. Without something onto which you can attach your idea of who you are, confusion and feelings of incompleteness result. Like Steve L., who has not developed his vision in any meaningful and productive way, you are not seaworthy. You are incapable of leaving the harbour, let alone sailing forth toward your destiny.

What you need is to put yourself in drydock and make yourself more seaworthy. Your meaning and purpose is that stable framework to which you can rebuild your identity and relaunch yourself anew. Only when you can float above the turmoil of life are you able to orientate yourself and set sail toward your destiny.

Vickie T., for instance, sees herself as an inspirational teacher. Not a teacher that educates children in a classroom at school, but a life teacher. One that helps autistic children and their parents learn the essential sets of life-skills they need to cope with the unique challenges they face. Her vision of who she is and what she wants to achieve has also established the role she needs to perform. It's given her direction, a frame of reference to rely on, and a role to fulfil.

With that role also comes meaning and purpose. She feels needed and wanted, she feels she can contribute to other people and make a positive difference to their lives. It motivates her to keep doing what she's doing, to keep fighting the good fight.

For this is the secret Vickie has stumbled upon:

> *Direction and purpose are two sides of the same coin: Your purpose gives your life direction, and your direction gives your life purpose.*

Because Steve L. has no such vision of himself or his future, he has no clear direction, no stable frame of reference, no definable role for his life. He therefore lacks purpose and meaning. He feels lost, disorientated. He doesn't know what he's supposed to do with himself and with his time. Life seems pointless and meaningless. He doesn't feel needed or wanted, rather ignored and useless, even a nuisance. He doesn't feel as if he contributes to society, and he certainly doesn't feel as if he makes a difference to anyone's life. He feels as if he's just another number, undervalued and unimportant.

Sadly, if things don't change, if Steve doesn't find or create a purpose for himself, he may well spend the next thirty or so years until retirement still feeling the way he does now and wondering why others succeeded and he didn't.

Imagine, though, if Steve took a leaf out of Vickie's book and began to use the principles of Life Leadership? Imagine the change in his life, the possibilities that would present to him. Imagine how successful his life could be.

He would set sail over the horizon to a limitless future.

LIFE SKILL #2: WHY

THE EVOLUTION OF YOU

Whether you like the adage or not, we're all on a journey. Even if we live in the same house for the whole of our life, we are all journeying forward.

Change dictates that. No matter how similar, no two days are the same. You change, your friends change, your family changes, events change, the world changes. The experience of change establishes the journey from what used to be, to what is now, to what will be. The pace of change may differ for everyone, but no matter how fast or how slow you experience change you are still moving forward from past to present to future.

Life Leaders make that journey an exciting adventure. They make it a remarkable quest. They don't wait for the right time or the right set of circumstances. They don't wait for the right person or right job. They take immediate action.

You have everything you need right now to make your life what you want. Hellen Keller discovered this truth:

> *Security is mostly a superstition. It does not exist in nature, nor do the children of men as a whole experience it. Avoiding danger is no safer in the long run than outright exposure... Life is a daring adventure or nothing at all.*[25]

Most people do not suffer the disabilities that Helen Keller suffered, yet most do not seek daring adventures or live their life to the fullest. But how can you start to live with freedom and adventure over and above everything else?

You need a vision.

Your vision establishes your life direction, of where you are now and where you want to be in the future. Your life direction creates your purpose, your reason for being. It's your cause. Your *quest*.

---

[25] Helen Keller, *The Open Door*, Doubleday N.Y., 1957

IT'S UP TO YOU!

It has been said that a life without a cause is a life without effect. If you don't have a cause in which you believe in, your impact is limited and your value to others is minimal.

But once you've established your cause, once you've identified the vision quest you're on, remarkable things start to happen. You get buy-in from others who also believe in your cause. They offer to help you, work for you, donate financially, because your cause also gives them purpose and meaning, hope and belief. They open doors that were previously closed or hidden to you. They have your back in times of trouble. They advocate for you. They thrive on the natural enthusiasm that comes from building something bigger than themselves. Your victory is their victory.

Other alchemy happens too. You change for the better. You become imbued with newness and freshness. You become exceedingly motivated. You stop living life by the book and become more flexible. You modify your expectations. You become more daring. You try new things. You adapt. You open yourself to new ideas, new formulas, new people. You become utterly centred, immovably so, with the surety of knowing that you are on the right track—that in fact there is *no other track*—that your vision quest is something of immense value and worth to the world.

Your focus intensifies too. Everything you do and think about is designed to help you move toward your vision of who you are and where you want to be. With a vision quest you are like water. A trickle at first, then a stream, then a river, flowing inexorably to the ocean, your destiny.

Life, in fact, becomes a daring adventure.

6 LIFE SKILL #3: WHAT

WHAT DO YOU WANT?

A VISION QUEST requires you to know who you are and to identify your cause, why you do what you do. It also requires that you know precisely what you want, which is Life Skill #3–What. This is the final building block of your 'I Am' axis at green diamond level, and the second building block of your 'I Will' axis at blue diamond level (see *Figure 9: The Diamond Triangle—Life Leadership Skills*).

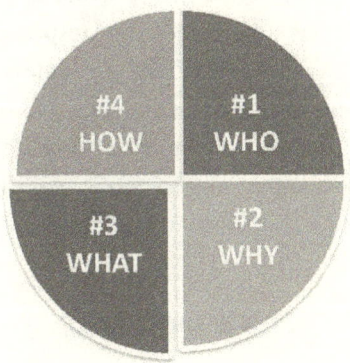

FIGURE 12:   Life Skill #3–What

It's surprising the number of people who don't know what they want or what they want to achieve. They know what they *don't* want, but like Steve L., who drifts day to day without direction, many people struggle with identifying what they want to do or where they want to be in five, ten, or even twenty years' time. What they want is vague and uncertain, their mind foggy and easily distracted.

IT'S UP TO YOU!

Some simply can't make a decision. There's too much choice. They get overwhelmed by the decision-making process and ultimately choose not to decide on anything. They have what's known as 'decision paralysis'. For these people, the fence sitters, no choice is the best choice.

Others may not be overwhelmed by choice, but they fear the responsibility of making a decision. Trevor K. is one such person. A great worker in the office, Trevor is the go-to man for anything that needs doing. Got a report that needs finalising before the end of the week? Trevor K. will get it done. Need to retrieve some computer files that have mysteriously gone missing? Trevor K. will find them for you. Heck, he'll even fix the office coffee machine if it's broken. He'll do almost anything you ask him to do. Just don't ask him to make a decision. Anything that requires a choice between two or more options, he fails miserably. He won't commit to any office decision because he has a distinct fear of responsibility.

But in life you can't avoid decisions. At some point responsibility lands in your lap and demands ownership. Nor can you sit on the fence forever. Complacency is not an option if you're committed to the Life Leadership journey, and so too is avoiding decisions.

So be brave, take responsibility, and choose what you want.

RESPONSIBLE CHOICE

The act of choosing requires you to be crystal clear about who you are and where you're going. It requires having 20/20 vision and precise direction. It requires tunnel vision, to be so focussed you can't be distracted by what other people think or say about you.

That's why you need to be brave. Because you might alienate people close to you. You might lose the support of friends and family who don't agree with your new direction and the new choices you make. It might mean you walk alone for a period of time. It might mean you get left out in the cold for a while.

LIFE SKILL #3: WHAT

Then again, it might not. Your friends and family will probably embrace your new choices. When they understand exactly what you're trying to achieve, when they see the vision you have of yourself, they'll probably want to support you in any way they can. They'll want to see you achieve your personal brand of success as much as you do.

Which is why you also need to be responsible. Your vision will encompass more than just you. It will outgrow you. It will become bigger than you. You will have the responsibility of doing whatever it takes to make your vision a reality because others will be riding on your success too. In many ways, your personal brand of success is like a child—it requires responsible parenting to grow and thrive. As its parent, you have responsibility for its being.

You will therefore want to make sure you get it right. You will need that crystal-clear vision of how you see yourself, as well as the precise direction in which you want your life to move forward.

YOUR VISION, YOUR MISSION

Blurred and hazy vision is a common problem. Not the kind of blurred vision that requires a prescription for corrective lenses, rather the blurred vision of who you are and what you want to achieve. If this is something you're struggling with, don't worry. You're not alone. This issue is in fact one of the main reasons this book has come into existence: to help you get clarity of who and what you want to be and achieve the success you want.

Your vision is blurred when you say or think things like:

- ♦ 'I don't know who I want to be or what I want to do.'
- ♦ 'I'm not sure I'm on the right track.'
- ♦ 'I really have no idea where I want to be in five years' time.'
- ♦ 'I want to do something else, but I don't know what.'

Thankfully, blurred vision can be cured. If you find yourself in a situation where your future is foggy and your direction is uncertain, then your mission is to get clarity about your vision. Your vision *is* your mission, in other words.

For instance, my vision is to be an expert in Life Leadership. That's my cause, to help people fulfil their amazing potential. To become who they were born to be and do what they were meant to do—to help people who feel stuck in a rut to find direction and live the life they always wanted. That's what I want to be known for. My mission to achieve that vision is to help 5000 people like yourself reach black diamond mastery within the next 15 years.

So a useful exercise to get clarity on your vision and mission is to ask yourself this question: What do I want to be famous for?

This requires identifying your value and worth: your value to yourself, your value to your family, your value to your work, your value to your community. This isn't monetary value, it's the value that only you can bring to the table. What is it that only you can be and do?

It will help to consider the difference between product and commodity. For instance, Coca Cola sells black fizzy drinks, but that's not their product, that's their commodity. Their product is *happiness*. They are in the industry of selling joy and happiness to the world. The black fizzy drink is just the means (commodity) by which they deliver happiness (product).

If you are a parent, the money you earn through your work is your commodity. The product you provide your family is safety, education, entertainment, nurture, health, joy, and so forth. You can drill this down to one word: wellbeing.

That's just one role you perform. You have many roles in your personal and working life, and it's a good exercise to work out the product you provide in each role. That's where your value is. For instance, in the Life Leaders Club, my role is to provide clarity through the process of The Diamond Triangle (commodity) for you to achieve personal success and prosperity (product). The Diamond Triangle is how you get clarity. Clarity is the means by which you achieve success and prosperity.

Once you've identified your vision and mission, the next step is to break down what you need to do into manageable goals.

TAGS—TARGETS, AIMS, GOALS

Goal setting is an important aspect of Life Skill #3–What. The adage of 'How do you eat an elephant?' sums this up best: one bite at a time. Setting Targets, Aims and Goals (TAGs) helps to break down your vision and mission into bite-sized chunks. TAGs help take the overwhelm out of what you need to do to achieve your big picture vision.

One of the habits of Life Leadership is to write down your goals and read your list every day. Brian Tracey, motivational speaker and author of *Eat that Frog!*,[26] says we should 'think on paper'. This is because writing down your goals employs both hemispheres of your brain, the creative right brain and the logical left brain.

In *Figure 13: Left & Right Brain*, the corpus callosum is the central bundle of nerves that connects the two hemispheres. Without the corpus callosum, the left and right brain cannot communicate with each other. Setting goals utilises your creative imagination to envisage your future requirements (right brain) and uses your rational logic to work out the steps and strategies required to achieve it (left brain). If you don't write down your goals and only keep them in your head, you are only utilising one half of your brain and thereby minimising your chances of success by at least 50%.

Writing your goals on paper, however, utilises your whole brain and maximises the chances of completing them. Research by psychologists at Dominican University, USA, in 2007

---

[26] *Eat that Frog!* by Brian Tracey, Berrett-Koehler, 2001

demonstrated that the act of writing goals enhances the achievement of those goals.[27] Those who wrote down their goals accomplished significantly more than those who did not. The same study also showed positive benefits of accountability and commitment in the successful achievement of intended goals.

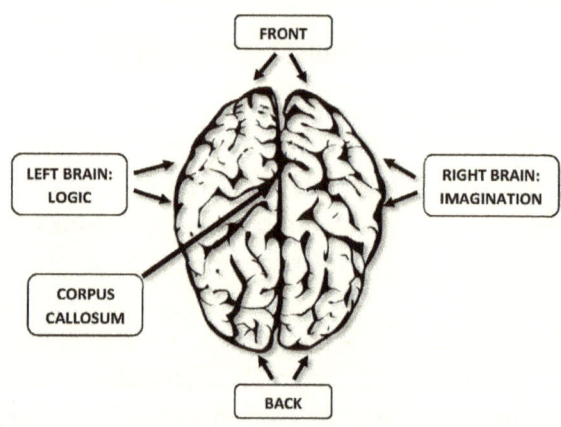

FIGURE 13:   Left & Right Brain

You are therefore more likely to achieve your goals and dreams when you set goals, think on paper, are committed, and held accountable for your actions to achieve them.

Pardon the pun, but setting goals is a no-brainer. In my Life Leadership coaching and mentoring program, I teach that GOALS:

-> **G**enerate motivation

-> **O**vercome obstacles

-> **A**ccount for action

-> **L**everage time, money, resources, and effort

-> **S**pecify results

---

[27] https://web.archive.org/web/20100610211058/http://www.dominican.edu/academics/ahss/psych/faculty/fulltime/gailmatthews/

LIFE SKILL #3: WHAT

G: Generate Motivation

Your goals must mean something to you, otherwise you won't be motivated to achieve them. In *Part 4: Tier #2: Success* we will discuss the types of goals that have the best outcomes for your Life Leadership journey. These will be the categories of goals that will help motivate and keep you on track to achieve what you want to achieve, like relationships, health, and career.

O: Overcome Obstacles

Goals also help you overcome the obstacles that you can expect to encounter on your Life Leadership journey. When you know your destination (vision), you can work backwards to set out the mission and goals you need to achieve your vision.

Start with the end in mind and you can anticipate the obstacles you'll face along your journey.

A: Account for Action

Accountability is another important function of goal setting. Having a Life Leadership mentor to hold you accountable to do the things you say you will do is a great thing to have. When you are held accountable, you are less likely to procrastinate and more likely to take the action you are meant to take. Accountability stems from the word 'account', which means to tally up, to keep score. Goal setting helps you to keep score of the things you need to do to achieve your vision. If you don't have an accountability coach, like a Life Leadership mentor, goals are a good substitute.

L: Leverage Time, Money, Resources, and Effort

Archimedes, the ancient Greek mathematician, is cited as saying, 'Give me a lever long enough and a fulcrum on which to place it, and I'll move the world.'

Levers give you leverage, the ability to move large objects with minimal strength. So too goals leverage your time, money, resources, and effort to achieve what you want to achieve. Through leverage, goals save you money and time, and improve your efficiency and effectiveness.

S: Specify Results

Focus, concentration, clarity, these are the qualities of Life Leadership and the trademarks of success. By specifying the results you want to achieve, goals also give you clarity and focus. Especially when you think on paper. Being specific in your outcomes enables you to laser target the results you want to achieve.

As stated earlier, my mission is to help 5000 people like yourself reach black diamond mastery within the next 15 years. Breaking that mission into goals, that's on average 330 people beginning the Life Leadership journey per year. Which is about 6-7 per week.

If we can achieve more, that'd be great. However, the point is to know what you want to achieve with as much clarity as you can. The next step is to work out how you go about doing it.

7 LIFE SKILL #4: HOW

HOW CAN YOU?

THE FIRST THREE Life Skills identify who you are, why you do what you do, and what you want to do. These skills give you a vision of who you want to be, the direction you want to take, and the milestones you need to reach to keep you on track. Now you need an action plan to put things into motion. Life Skill #4–How, is the first building block of your 'I Can' axis at brown diamond level, and the final building block of your 'I Will' axis at white diamond level (see *Figure 9: The Diamond Triangle—Life Leadership Skills*).

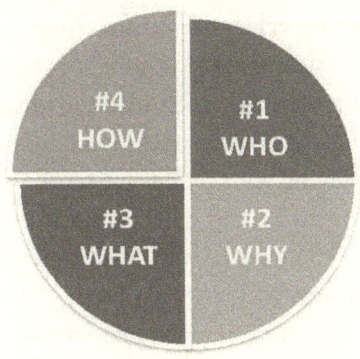

FIGURE 14:   Life Skill #4–How

If you fail to plan, you plan to fail, as they say. So before you take any action, you should first set aside some time to plan what it is you are going to do and how you are going to do it.

Mapping your journey requires knowledge of where you are

now and where you want to get to. It also requires a timeframe of when you want to achieve your vision, mission, and goals (which is why this life skill also encompasses your 'where and when').

Your timeframe is usually set out in years, months, weeks, and days. Classical action plans are set out as such:

-> 3 - 5 years	-> 60 days
-> 1 year	-> 30 days
-> 180 days	-> Weekly
-> 90 days	-> Daily

As a Life Leader, you will be expected to have a vision of where you want to be in 5 years. This big picture vision allows you to work back and establish what you want your life to look like in 3 years, just over halfway along your journey. This makes it easier to think about where you would like to be at in a year's time, and then in 6 months or 180 days. From here you can get very specific about what goals need to be achieved within 90, 60, and 30 days, and actively set and complete weekly and daily goals.

Let's assume you want to reach black diamond mastery in 18-24 months, a realistic vision. It takes this amount of time because Life Leadership is 'living your being'. It's more than just putting on paper who you want to be and what you want to do and thinking that the job's done. You have to walk your talk, and this takes time, not to mention slip-ups and obstacles along the way.

Realistically, within one year you can aspire to ascend to blue diamond level. In the first 3-4 months, you will be finishing orange diamond level and getting to brown diamond level.

This allows you to plan the next 180 days, breaking it down into 90, 60, 30-day goals. When we discuss Life Leadership Practices in the following chapters, you will be given exercises to set goals on a daily and weekly basis.

LIFE SKILL #4: HOW

TAKING ACTION

You have now established your vision, mission, goals, and action plan. Without executing the plan, however, it will remain a wishful dream. This is now the time of active doing, the implementation of the silent, but no less effective, 4th Rule of Success—Deliver It. Without action there is no success. Without the habit of doing there is no prosperity. As the saying goes, an ounce of action is worth a pound of theorising.

Motivation and discipline are key to taking action. Which is why purpose and meaning are so important, to keep you motivated on your journey and to instil the commitment and discipline you need to do what's required every day. Like going to the gym or following a weight loss program, when you do at least one thing every day to accomplish your goals it soon becomes a habit, and habits achieve results.

When the space shuttle blasted into orbit, 80% of its fuel was burned in the first two minutes of take-off. This initial sequence was always the hardest and most dangerous part of the launch. After it had broken free of the earth's gravity, it settled into orbit with the inertia it had established through this initial phase. From then on, it needed very little fuel to complete the mission.

Like the space shuttle, 80% of your effort will be in the initial phase of your Life Leadership journey. If you want to reach the stars, you will need to break free from the gravity pulling you back to your normal, everyday life, the life that you are trying change for the better. That pull is the pull of your neomammalian, paleomammalian and reptilian brain—your beliefs, emotions, and instincts.

Habit is what will build your momentum through the initial phase of your journey. Being motivated, committed, and disciplined will maintain your inertia, which means you will need less energy to complete your mission. This is where the self-perpetuating system of The Diamond Triangle kicks in.

But if you fall out of the habit of doing something every day to achieve your mission, your momentum will slow and your progress will come to a halt.

Then you will have to relaunch, which will require more effort and energy than had you maintained your habit.

STRUCTURE, STRATEGIES & SYSTEMS

Tradesmen are only as good as the tools they use. Your toolkit affects the quality of your work and the timeframe in which you complete your project. Poor tools either function poorly or not at all and add to the frustration of your work. If you spend half your time fixing broken tools or putting up with substandard equipment, then a lot of your focus is diverted away from your project and your time is wasted.

Life Leadership structure, strategies, and systems are specialised tools to employ along your journey to success and prosperity. The Life Leadership Model of orange to purple diamond level is the framework or structure of your journey. First you identify your level, then you employ the necessary strategies to achieve the life skills you need to ascend to the next level. Essential to your strategy are the systems and processes you use.

As Bill Gates said in an interview with *Time Magazine* in 2018:

> *If you want to improve something, look for ways to build better systems.*

For instance, one of our goals in the Life Leaders club is to have at any given time 1,500 active and engaged email subscribers. This goal is required to complete our bigger goal of helping 330 people per year begin the Life Leadership journey to black diamond mastery, and our overall mission of 5000 within 15 years.

To achieve our email subscriber goals, we need to devise a strategy and implement an emailing system. We employ a digital marketing strategy to attract visitors and readers to our website through social media advertising, posts, blogs, podcasts, videos, and other online activities. Visitors arriving on our website are given the opportunity to sign up to our regular newsletters. To entice them to sign up, we offer a great value ebook they can read for free. In this ebook they can get a taste of what Life Leadership is all about, such as the Life Leadership Model, The Diamond Triangle, and the 4 Tenets of Success. Once they've signed up, they receive regular emails with loads of valuable resources and information, along with subscriber-only offers for discounts to Life Leadership courses and membership.

We need systems to build our subscriber list, such as Mailchimp, Aweber, and Infusionsoft to automate our emails and warehouse our database. We also need a professional website to integrate our subscriber and membership platforms, and we need social media platforms to direct traffic to our website and build our online communities.

But at the end of the day, all our strategies and systems are designed to do one thing: to facilitate a face-to-face meeting with me or one of our Life Leadership mentors. If this can't happen in the same physical location, we will use Skype or Zoom or even a phone call. The important thing is that we establish a human connection, and all our systems are developed to make this happen.

Which brings us to the people in your world.

PEOPLE POWER

Psychologists claim that you are the product of the five people you most associate with. Your social connections are enormously influential on your sense of self. Be very particular, then, about who you spend most time with. They are extremely influential on who you become, your wellbeing, your happiness, and the level of success you achieve.

This is due in part to the psychological phenomenon of social influence. This is the way in which an individual shapes their ideas, thoughts, and behaviours to conform to a social group or to a position of authority. You encounter social influence every day at home, at work, and with friendship groups. Social influence is a powerful influence on how you think and behave. For instance, a person opposed to guns and who is an advocate for stronger gun laws can, over time, change their view if they spend long enough in the company of others who believe in the right to bear arms.

One reason we conform is our human need to belong and to be accepted. We want to fit in and be liked and respected. You can even find yourself wearing the same types of clothing and adopting the same mannerisms of your group. You can begin to speak like them, react like them, and before you know it you are just like them. This type of conformity is known as normative social influence.

The people you associate with are also a means of support and cooperation, especially when working to achieve a common goal. A collective goal bonds the group in a way other activities don't, reinforcing the tribal idea that 'you're one of us now'.

No one is an island, and you will need others to help you achieve your personal brand of success. Part of the Life Leadership journey is therefore to decide who you allow to influence you. Choose wisely. Surround yourself with people who share the philosophies and values that you want to aspire and adhere to, like those who are also on a journey of self-improvement.

Be very aware, then, of how others influence you and how you influence others. Because you will become like them, and they will become like you.

That's people power.

LIFE SKILL #4: HOW

THE MASTERMIND

Life leaders also know that other people have the power to help you become a success through the principle known as The Mastermind. This principle was first described by Napoleon Hill in his book, *The Law of Success*,[28] whereby he describes how some of the most successful people in history ascribed their success to this principle—Henry Ford, Alexander Graham Bell, Theodore Roosevelt, Thomas Edison, and John D. Rockefeller.

Walt Disney, too, became hugely successful due, in large part, to his ability to gather the right people around him, like Ub Iwerks, the cartoonist who helped create the character Mickie Mouse. Although Disney suffered early losses and the bankruptcy of Laugh-O-Grams Studios, he became a pioneer of the American animation industry and creator the Disney Brothers Studio (later, The Walt Disney Company) because of his ability to inspire those around him to work in collaboration toward a common goal.

A mastermind is created whenever two or more people get together to problem solve in a spirit of collaboration and mutual intent. It's a case of 1 + 1 = 3, where the sum is greater than its parts, where a 'bigger mind' is created through the combination of the minds in the mastermind group. The more individual minds present, the bigger and more powerful the mastermind created. Researchers suggest an optimal size of eight to ten people, and that these people should meet regularly to maximise the effect of the mastermind.

A properly created mastermind follows the same 3 Golden Rules of The Diamond Triangle—Defining, Determining, Designing—to answer the Who, Why, What, and How questions:

-> Who are the best people to create the mastermind?

-> Why does the mastermind need to exist: What is its purpose, it's reason for being?

---

[28] Napoleon Hill, *The Law of Success*, Ralston University Press, 1925

-> What is the intention of the mastermind?

-> How is the intended outcome going to be achieved?

FIGURE 15: The Mastermind

To create a mastermind that's beneficial and effective for all who are involved with it, four considerations are necessary:

1. The Right People.
2. Harmonious Agreement.
3. Clarity of Vision.
4. Purpose and Belief.

The Right People

There are two types of mastermind: one which focuses on an individual's success, and another that focusses on the success of all the individuals in the group.

It's therefore important to know from the very beginning who you want to be part of your mastermind group. If the intent of creating the mastermind is for your own success, you will need to gather people who want to help you achieve your goals. Surround yourself with generals who want your success as much as they want their own.

LIFE SKILL #4: HOW

This is why having a mentor is so valuable. A good mentor understands the power of the mastermind and how to harness its power with focus and intent for your benefit.

If the intent of creating the mastermind is for the success of everybody, then it's important that the group's time and resources are distributed and allocated equally. If one person dominates the group, or others are not as engaged and involved with helping others achieve their aims, then the mastermind will not function optimally.

Harmonious Agreement

A mastermind is more than just an office meeting or a soundboarding session. The emphasis is on agreement: the power of the mastermind comes from having all involved agreeing to work together in harmony for a united outcome.

Even if one person in the mastermind group fails to work in the spirit of collaboration and secretly harbours an opposing intention, it greatly diminishes the mastermind's power to manifest the desired outcome.

A mastermind created by harmonious agreement, however, is a powerful force.

Clarity of Vision

Think of a mastermind as a highly intensive focus group, where everyone in the group has gathered with the same intent. As with a focus group, a mastermind works best with a facilitator.

For a mastermind created to help an individual achieve their goals, this facilitator should lead the group in the direction of the intended outcome and have the trust of everyone present. The facilitator should also have the ability to clearly describe their vision so that the others have a clear picture of the definitive aim of the mastermind, and that all agree the mastermind is working to achieve this aim.

For a mastermind created for the benefit of everyone in the group, a rotating leadership or facilitator is recommended. Each individual should have a clear and concise vision so that everybody present understands what they are trying to achieve and what their current challenges are to manifest that vision.

Purpose and Belief

For a mastermind to succeed in its created intention, each individual must feel, trust and believe that the mastermind will be of mutual benefit to everybody in the group. A mastermind not founded on a win-win agenda will struggle from the very outset.

This is why it's important to have a clearly defined and understood reason for the mastermind to exist. The mastermind needs a cause for everyone to believe in, whatever that cause may be. A cause gets buy in from its members. They are willing to invest their time, money, emotions, expertise, and efforts into manifesting that cause into a reality.

Without belief in the underlying purpose of the mastermind, it will lack energy and impetus, and soon its momentum will slow to a standstill.

All successful mastermind sessions also end with a plan for action. Without implementing the strategies and systems that arise from the session, very little will be achieved and the benefits of the mastermind will be lost or wasted.

Action amplifies the power of the mastermind. Inaction neutralises it.

* * *

LIFE SKILL #4: HOW

We will now discuss the 9 Life Leadership Practices through the levels of the Life Leadership program. Each practice has one or more exercises for you to complete before moving onto the next level.

I now invite you to take action and begin the journey of Life Leadership mastery.

PART 3

LIFE LEADERSHIP PRACTICES

TIER #1: FOCUS

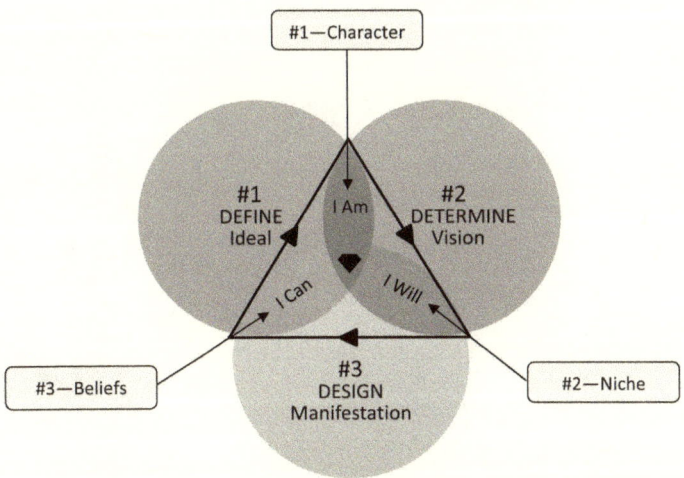

8 ORANGE DIAMOND: BUILD YOUR CHARACTER

LIFE LEADERSHIP PRACTICE #1

Your Life Leadership journey begins at orange diamond level. The aim of this level is to attain focus-level knowledge of Life Skill #1–Who, and progress to brown diamond level within 3-4 months. The practice of building your character is the first in the process of 'Reconnecting' and moving into Quadrant #1 on the Empowered Living Index.

The core of this Life Leadership Practice is to define that ideal vision of who you want to be and to build your ideal character. In The Diamond Triangle, your character is analogous to the capstone of a pyramid. There are two more building blocks of your 'I Am' axis, which we will discuss later, but for now The Diamond Triangle looks like this:

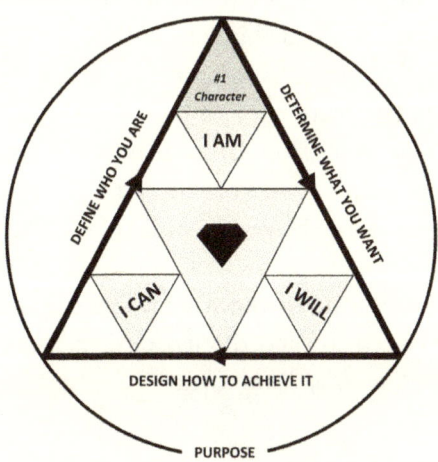

FIGURE 16:   Orange Diamond—Character

THE TEST OF CHARACTER

We have previously mentioned some of the greatest people that have ever lived—Winston Churchill, Mahatma Gandhi, Mother Teresa, Nelson Mandela, Jesus. When we think about these people, what is their attraction? It isn't money. It isn't the positions of power they held. It isn't even their fame. So, what is their allure?

What these people had was strength of character. Money talks, but it's character that earns your respect. These people were heroic. They had devotion to principle, an unwavering commitment to the causes they believed in.

In *The Law of Success*, Napoleon Hill emphasises the vital importance of developing your character:

> *There is but one thing in the world that gives us real and enduring power, and that is* character... *If you would be a person of great influence, then be a person of real character.*[29]

Greatness is rooted in a deep and unshakeable faith in the principle of truth. The great characters of history were not defined by what they did or the circumstances in which they lived. They were defined by the truth of who they were, and this they took responsibility to define themselves. This is a responsibility we all share. You must define who you are lest somebody else does it for you. You must take the responsibility of saying, 'This is who I am!'

Wallace Wattles, one of the forefathers of the New Thought Movement over a century ago, discussed the nature of great people in his book, *The Science of Being Great*:

---

[29] Napoleon Hill, *The Law of Success*, Ralston University Press, 1925

ORANGE DIAMOND: BUILD YOUR CHARACTER

> *We see it... in every man and woman who has attained a place on the muster roll of the great ones of the world. Faith—not a faith in one's self or in one's own powers but faith in principle; Something Great which upholds right... Without this faith it is not possible for anyone to rise to real greatness. The man who has no faith in principle will always be a small man.*[30]

You will need to consider, then, what part of your character you want to develop and strengthen. How do you want others to see you? What do you want others to say about you? What is your principle, your truth?

But first, to work on your character you must define what it is, otherwise you won't know what to improve and what to jettison. The great people in history can point you in the right direction. Although they may seem superhuman, they're not, which means their feats and endeavours are just benchmarks of human capabilities. So, if they can do it, if they can achieve greatness of character, so too can you.

Because here's the truth about character:

Great character isn't genetic; it is learned and cultivated.

Nor is great character only for the privileged. Very few of history's great characters were born into wealthy, well-to-do families. Most grew up in humble circumstances. They endured hardships of one form or another throughout their life, but it didn't break them. It moulded them into the great character and person they became. Mandela admitted that incarceration made him let go of hate and forced him to grow up. Gandhi's experience with racism taught him that violence was not the answer to liberating his nation. Churchill's disastrous failings in

---

[30] Wallace Wattles, *The Science of Being Great*, Elizabeth Towne, 1910

World War 1 helped develop the leadership qualities needed to facedown Hitler two decades later.

Character is developed, and it's usually developed in the School of Hard Knocks. But if you want something bad enough, if you really want to achieve something with every fibre of your body, life will test you to see if you're ready. It will test your skills, it will test your ability to perform under pressure, but most of all it will test your strength of character. It does this by putting you in situations of duress.

Weightlifters only know how strong they are by lifting weights. Adding five kilograms to their best lift sets a new benchmark. Can they do it? Can they lift more than before? They'll only know by doing it, testing the limits of their capabilities. They either set a new personal best or they don't.

So too your career path, where you are generally promoted to the level of your incapability. Your superiors can only know what you're capable of by setting you work that's above your current skill level. This may feel awkward and outside your comfort zone, but it's the only way your employer knows what you're capable of. Either you're successful in the work and get the desired result, then get another promotion to the next level, or you fail the test and remain at that current level of employment. Either way, a benchmark is set. You will rise through the ranks and settle at the level where your skills are incapable of performing the role to which you've been promoted, and there you will stay until you upskill and improve your capabilities or move on to another place of employment.

Strength of character is likewise tested. Life often asks you to lift more than you think you can, or it asks you to perform to a level outside your comfort zone. This is a good thing, not a bad thing. Life is an education. It is continually examining who and what you claim to be.

This is the Science of Life. As with all scientific advancement, if a theory can't be tested against nature and verified with observable results, it remains just a theory, an idea. This is why Life tests you—so that you can prove to yourself you can be the best version you can imagine. Your ideal you needs testing and verifying to manifest and become real. Which, like all examination of character, is hard and difficult. But here's the reality that most wish were not true:

Life isn't meant to be easy.

To wish that life was easy and plain sailing is to miss the point. Circumstances are not designed to give you comfort and pleasure, but to test you. It's meant to be difficult. The quicker you accept this, the quicker you will overcome your obstacles to your success and prosperity. Get comfortable with being uncomfortable. Embrace the challenge. Embrace the examination. Let it work for you, not against you. It's designed to build your character.

As the African proverb reminds us, calm waters never made a good sailor. A test of a strong character is therefore in the response to being tested—strong characters welcome the trial because they know it's the act of testing and being examined that builds their strength. Weak personalities shy away from examination of their character because at heart they know they're weak and underprepared. A weightlifter doesn't fear the weights; he actively seeks them as a test to his strength. An employee keen for promotion doesn't shy away from difficult projects; she routinely volunteers as a test to her capabilities.

Yet, as James Allen pointed out:

> *Men are anxious to improve their circumstances, but are unwilling to improve themselves; they therefore remain bound.*[31]

Building strong character therefore involves actively seeking

---

[31] James Allen, *As a Man Thinketh*, Thomas Y. Crowell Co., 1902

out tests to improve and develop yourself, lest you remain bound to your current set of circumstances. If you're not challenged, you can't change for the better and your circumstances won't improve.

So seek to continually improve your character, or risk being left behind.

THE EVOLUTION OF CHARACTER

Life Leaders make sure they aren't left behind. They actively adapt to change and deliberately take advantage of it. They know that strength isn't remaining the same as they've always been; it's the ability to adapt and grow, to evolve into something superior than what you have previously been. You are both 'becoming' (outward) and 'being' (inner) while you build your character.

In the past, adaptability made humans the most successful creatures on earth. Our unique ability to adjust to circumstances meant we increased our chances of survival. In fact, we did more than just survive, we thrived. Fortunately, we still retain this unique capability. It is still part of our genetic makeup. Which is wonderful news, because your adaptability also increases your chances of success in today's world. But only if you use it. The more adaptable you are, the more likely you will become successful at what you do and the more likely you'll become the person you wish to be.

In the battle between the rock and the river, the river always wins. The power of water lies in its non-resistance and changeability. A mountain, though, no matter how mighty, eventually gets eroded. The ocean, too, like the river, adapts to its circumstances. As a body of water, the ocean is the epitome of birth and rebirth. It loses part of itself through evaporation, then it is cleansed and replenished when that evaporation condenses and falls back to earth. Its strength lies in utilising the process of change and transformation. For this reason, the oceans have been on earth far longer than any of the oldest mountains.

ORANGE DIAMOND: BUILD YOUR CHARACTER

Life Leaders are therefore oceans with depth, capable of adapting to their circumstances. They are not steadfast mountains. Even losses (failures) are evaporated and eventually replenished, strengthening their character, making them bigger and better than they were before. One of their mottos is:

I never lose; I either win or I learn.

As we've been reiterating throughout this book, your personal brand of success is dependent on defining who and what you are. Want to hitch your wagon to a star? Great, but you'll need to develop your character as you go, or you'll only rise to the level that your character is incapable of.

So, yes, hitch your wagon to a star, dream big, *be* big. But remember this:

The beauty of embarking towards far off destinations and setting high goals to achieve is so that your character grows and develops along the journey.

These are some of the riches you find on your journey to Ithaca. Your ability to stay the course, however, is enhanced by your capacity to endure. That's why it's said that success is 10% inspiration and 90% perspiration. You build your mental strength and resilience with strength of character, with determination and willpower; perseverance and persistence; patience and courage; single-mindedness and focus.

A quick exercise you can do right now is to rate your overall mental strength and resolve on a scale of 1-10 (1 being the lowest and 10 being the highest). If you rate your score below 6, this is probably an area you need to work on. The good news is, just as physical strength can be improved through a physical fitness regime, your mental strength and endurance can be improved through a mental fitness regime, such as meditation, positive affirmations, life-coaching, mindfulness, and present moment focusing.

START AT THE END

In defining your character, one question many people ask is: 'Where do I start?'

This is a great question because it means the person asking has identified that they want to change for the better. They want to grow into the bigger person they know they are. So, I tell them to start at the end.

The end, of course, being your funeral. The aim is to write your own eulogy, to imagine yourself standing before your mourners and telling them what a great person you were, how this world has been a better place for you having been alive. The idea is not to focus too much on your past achievements per se, but rather the character you had become and to tell the stories that reflected your strength of character.

Because, at the end, what is it that really matters? Does all the wealth and possessions you've accumulated matter to loved ones when you're dead? Of course not. It's the emotional memory of who you were that counts. The things you stood for, the values you held, the person you had become. The way you treated people. How you inspired others. The positive difference you made to the world. The love you gave.

Paying the bills, having a roof over your head, putting food on the table is, of course, important. That's not the issue at hand. There is something just as important as these, if not more important, and that's the investment you have in yourself. You pay the bills, great. You pay off the mortgage, great. You educate yourself, great.

ORANGE DIAMOND: BUILD YOUR CHARACTER

But how much do you invest in yourself? How much attention do you devote to developing your character? How much time do you spend thinking about the person you want to be and planning how to be that person? How much commitment do you have to *you*?

On your very last day, what matters is who you are, not how much stuff you own or how many dollars you have sitting in your bank account. Why? Because it's the only thing that's real, the only thing that has a permanent legacy. Memories are embedded with emotions and feelings; that's why people remember how you made them feel, and the stronger the emotion the stronger the memory. How, then, do you want people to remember you?

Writing your own eulogy is therefore a great exercise. It's a simple visualisation technique to help you get clarity with who you want to be. Like setting goals, when you start at the end, your funeral, you can work backwards to where you are now to identify the milestones you need to reach to get to your destination. Which, in this case, is your character. This exercise helps you to map your path to the person you want to be. Once you know your destination, you can plot the journey you need to take to get there, the things you need to do to make it happen, even the obstacles to avoid along the way.

So, what do you want others to say about you? Do you want to be wise? Do you want to be known as someone who was honest, who had integrity? Somebody who was reliable and trustworthy? Somebody who was generous and kind? Somebody who believed in a cause and never gave up, who always did what was right no matter what everyone else was doing around them?

There are others than these listed below in *Table 13: Positive Character Traits*, but here are some positive character traits you might like to choose from:

POSITIVE CHARACTER TRAITS	
Patience	Respectfulness
Honesty	Kindness
Loyalty	Perseverance
Humility	Authenticity
Responsibility	Generosity
Courage	Forgiveness
Wisdom	Gratefulness

TABLE 13:   Positive Character Traits

Remember though, whatever and whomever you decide you want to be, Life will test you. And it will test you immediately. Do you want to be patient and wise? Life will give you the opportunity to be patient and wise. Maybe you'll be forced to sit and wait in a traffic jam the next time you drive. Maybe someone will cut in front of you or deliberately block your path. What will you do? Will you be patient with that person, or will you fly into a furious rage at their behaviour?

Do you want to be known as somebody who is generous and kind? Life will give you the opportunity to be generous and kind. Maybe you'll see a drug addict or a beggar on the next corner you walk around. What will you do? Will you be generous and kind to that person, or will you judge them for the circumstances in which you believe they've brought upon themselves?

But take heed:

Your judgment of another is not a reflection of that person but a reflection of your own character.

ORANGE DIAMOND: BUILD YOUR CHARACTER

Think about that for a moment. Judgement of another says more about who you are than it does about them. It is an indicator as to who is controlling most of your thought processes, you or your triune brain?

There will be a thousand and more opportunities to express those traits you wish for yourself and to be the great character you can be. Every day will be an examination of the new you that you want to express. Not an examination to bring you down, to have you fail. Rather, an examination to build your strength, lift you up, to pass the test you've set yourself—to have great character.

So, use every opportunity to build your character, to make it bigger, to make it the best it can be. Because the strength of your character is the capstone of your personal brand of success.

IT'S UP TO YOU!

ORANGE DIAMOND PRACTICE—BUILD YOUR CHARACTER

Previously we discussed how you are the product of the five people you most associate with. Your first Life Leadership Practice will use this principle to build your character.

If you have an idea to start out in business, business coaches will advise you to build your network first, then build your business. Your network is the root system by which your business can grow and thrive. Without a solid network, a business lacks the underlying support it needs to survive and flourish.

Building your character is analogous to building your business network—it's the foundation upon which your personal brand of success is sustained. This Life Leadership Practice, 'Revive the Five', has been designed to give you that support structure:

1. Choose five ideal character strengths that you admire in others and would like to develop over the course of your life and be remembered for (use *Table 13: Positive Character Traits* for examples).

2. Now identify five great characters in history that embody each of these five ideal character strengths you have chosen.

3. Write down each historical figure representing each character strength on a piece of paper that you can read each morning before you head out and each night before you go to bed.[32]

4. For each historical figure, say these words each morning and evening for the next 30 days: *[Name of historical figure], I admire your [state character strength], and I am grateful for the power of [state*

---

[32] A printed picture or image of the historical figure will make this practice even more powerful.

ORANGE DIAMOND: BUILD YOUR CHARACTER

character strength] in achieving my own success and prosperity. I hereby ask for your guidance in becoming a person of [state character strength], which you so embodied.

5. Expect to be tested.

* * *

To help you with the Revive the Five exercise, I will share with you my five ideal character traits and the historical figures I associate them with (and of course, you can have as many as you like, you don't have to limit yourself to five):

#1: Abraham Lincoln, I admire your *integrity* and dedication to always doing what is right, and I am grateful for the *power of honesty* in achieving my own success and prosperity. I hereby ask for your guidance in becoming a person of *integrity* and chivalry who always stands up for the truth, which you so embodied.

#2: Mother Teresa, I admire your *faith* and dedication to humanity and helping the poor, and I am grateful for the *power of faith* in achieving my own success and prosperity. I hereby ask for your guidance in becoming a person of faith and *service to others*, which you so embodied.

#3: Winston Churchill, I admire your *tenacity* and never-give-up determination, and I am grateful for the *power of perseverance* in achieving my own success and prosperity. I hereby ask for your guidance in becoming a person of *determined will* who never gives up on his greater purpose, which you so embodied.

#4: Nelson Mandela, I admire your ability to transform hate into *forgiveness*, and I am grateful for the *power of forgiveness* in achieving my own success and prosperity. I hereby ask for your guidance in becoming a person of *forgiveness* and noble stature, which you so embodied.

#5: Jesus Christ, I admire your ultimate act of *self-sacrifice* and amazing love for humanity, and I am grateful for the *power of love* in achieving my own success and prosperity. I hereby ask for your guidance in becoming a person of selflessness and *unconditional love for humanity*, which you so embodied.

9 BROWN DIAMOND: FIND YOUR NICHE

LIFE LEADERSHIP PRACTICE #2

THE NEXT LEVEL of your Life Leadership journey is brown diamond. The aim of this level is to attain focus-level knowledge of Life Skill #2–Why, and progress to yellow diamond level within 3-4 months. The practice of finding your niche is the first in the process of 'Realigning' and moving into Quadrant #1 in the Empowered Living Index.

The core of this Life Leadership Practice is to find that place where you truly belong. In The Diamond Triangle, your niche is the first of three building blocks in your 'I Will' axis, and is now looking like this:

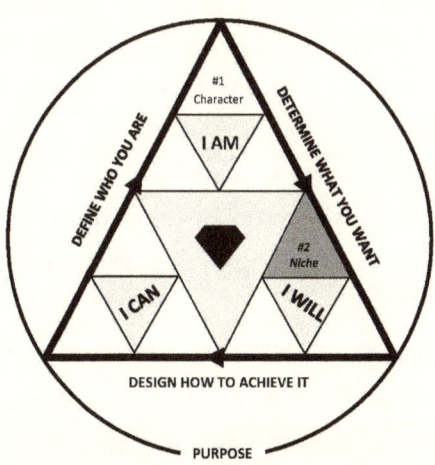

FIGURE 17: Brown Diamond—Niche

IT'S UP TO YOU!

WHAT'S YOUR THING?

You have a special place in this world that's unique to you and you alone, where *only you* fit perfectly. You know when you find it because you are filled with the steadfast assurance that this is exactly where you're meant to be, that there is no other place for you.

As a Life Leader, one of your top priorities is to find your niche, and the best place to start is to ask yourself this question: *What's my THING?*

This is one of the most important questions you can ever ask. It's vital, even, because when you know your thing, you will find your niche.

I'll say that again:

When you know your thing, you will find your niche.

Finding your niche in life need not be so difficult. Your niche is simply where:

- N: Your *Nature* or natural personality shines.
- I: Your *Intellectual* skillsets and capabilities are maximised (mental, emotional, physical, and spiritual).
- C: Your *Core Talents* are fully utilised and honed.
- H: Your *Heart* or passions are fulfilled and expressed.
- E: Your *Experience* builds to the levels of expertise and mastery.

As it turns out, your THING[33] and your NICHE are one and the same. Your THING is:

---

[33] In *The Purpose-driven Life: What on Earth am I Here For?*, Zondervan, 2002, Rick Warren talks about understanding your life-purpose specifically from a Christian perspective. Although similar, your THING differs in its secular approach to understanding your 'why' (although you may adapt it for spiritual or religious purposes as you wish).

BROWN DIAMOND: FIND YOUR NICHE

T: Your *Talent or talents*.
H: Your *Heart* or Passion.
I: Your *Intellectual* skillset and capabilities (mental, emotional, physical, and spiritual).
N: Your *Nature* or natural personality.
G: Your *General Experience*.

Your THING is not a 1-stop shop for all the solutions to all your life's problems, but it is your direction finder. It's like a compass pointing you toward your big picture vision. Keep track of it weekly, if not daily, so that you stay on course. Keep asking yourself, 'What's my *thing*?' and you will navigate your way to your niche.

I met Christine P. when she attended one of my Life Leadership courses, which ran over a 4-week period. She was a highly successful lawyer with a high wage to match. She enjoyed the lifestyle her career afforded, but she harboured a dream of starting her own business in retail. She had held onto this dream for over two decades, but her fear of losing her lifestyle and being forced to downsize wasn't appealing, so her dream remained just a dream.

Unfortunately, she was suffering an internal battle of 'should I, or shouldn't I?' Although retirement was still some years in the future, it was close enough for her to get nervous about. Christine was at the point where she either went ahead with her dream of owning her own business, or letting go of her dream forever.

When we discussed the idea of realigning with her Life Purpose and finding her niche, a light went off in her head. 'This is just the thing I needed to stop procrastinating!' she blurted. Several months on, she has begun the process of creating the business she has always dreamed of.

Your THING not only points you in the right direction, it also stops procrastination from stealing your most valuable asset—your time.

IT'S UP TO YOU!

T—YOUR TALENTS

Your talent is the gift you were born with. For many though, being 'gifted' is not something people believe they are. A gift is usually the reserve of famous actors, writers, artists, or sportspeople, not something they would normally attribute to themselves.

Although some people are more talented than others at some things, everyone is born with a talent, something they are naturally good at. Talents, though, are more than just the result of good genes. They are also not the result of what we have learned through our schooling and environment. Talents transcend genetics and our location. When nurtured with intent and effort, they are the seeds within us that grow into strong skillsets which can, over time, be mastered.

For some, it's the gift of storytelling or playing a musical instrument. For others, it's understanding numbers or languages. Some have a natural talent for sport. Others have a talent for acting, dancing, or writing. Some have great technical or scientific talents. Others work well with their hands, others with their minds. Some have the gift of empathy and understanding. Some have creative talents. Others see patterns in nature that others cannot fathom.

The list of talents is long and varied. If, however, you find it difficult to identify your talent, here are three exercises to help unearth the latent talent within you. They are: What's Your Midas Touch?, Trash or Treasure, and Talent Spotting.

#1: What's Your Midas Touch?

In the parable of King Midas, the king was granted his wish that everything he touched turned to gold. This initial blessing, however, quickly became a curse as things such as food and water, even people, were turned into gold.

Nonetheless, for our purposes, your talent can be found in the things you turn to gold with seeming ease. What is that activity?

BROWN DIAMOND: FIND YOUR NICHE

What is your Midas touch, the thing you do that very rarely fails?

Identify this and you identify the gold within you, your hidden talent.

#2: Trash or Treasure?

The way you talk to yourself can sometimes be negative and self-deprecating, so don't be your own worst enemy. Don't put yourself down and dismiss your value to others and those close to you. If you're not careful, you can start to believe you're not any good at anything, that you are a talentless individual with no hope in the world.

But that's not true. You do have a talent, one that you were born with, a treasure waiting for you to discover.

If you don't believe this, then don't listen to yourself. Listen instead to what others say of you. Others you trust, the people close to you. They know what you're good at. Ask them what they think your natural talents are. Ask them what qualities you have that they would like in themselves or are even a little envious of.

What is it that you make look easy? What job or career do they think you would be perfect for, and why do they think that?

They'll help you find the truth about your hidden talents and help you find your inner treasure.

#3: Talent Spotting

In professional sport, talent spotters and scouts scour the country and further afield to locate undiscovered talent for their club. Talent spotters watch hundreds of games, identifying young players that have the potential to develop into a professional player or elite athlete.

A talent spotter will have a checklist to lookout for in a player. They are athletic. They have stamina. They have balance. They show poise and a natural flair for the game. They can read the play. They have a precocious skillset highly developed for their age.

But they are not yet the real deal. They show great potential, but they still have a lot to learn to develop into a player of the future. Their potential needs to be honed and sharpened.

The word here is potential. Unrealised talent has the potential to develop into genuine talent, but first it needs to be recognised. Talent that goes unrecognised or ignored is wasted. A gift unopened cannot share its joy. A light switched off is forever in the dark.

Your job is to talent spot your own talent. It may help to write down a list of all the things you have always been good at doing. You'll probably find that there's one activity that you have always been naturally proficient, something that you've always done well without much thought or effort. This talent or gift is something you probably started noticing in early childhood. What is that thing? What is the one thing that has stood head and shoulders above everything else you've done? What is the thing that you can claim as your own, the one thing you can say, 'I've always been really good at this!'

Find this and you spot your hidden talent, the gift you were born with.

H—HEART & PASSIONS

Your Life Purpose can be felt as a physical force, and that force is passion. Passion is what your purpose feels like. When you feel passion, you feel *alive*. Because that's what passion is—the feeling of your life-force flowing through you, unencumbered and uninterrupted.

It's also what your purpose sounds like. When you hear the calling of your passion, you hear the calling of your purpose. For that's also what your purpose is, a calling. A vocation.

Like the talent you were born with, everyone has a passion for something and therefore everyone has a purpose. Everyone is called to be more than what they are now, to be something greater.

BROWN DIAMOND: FIND YOUR NICHE

Remember, your external success is the platform with which you, a Life Leader, have impact and influence on others. As such, what you do is of secondary importance to who you are. It is still important, but not as important as who you are being while you're doing what you do. Your passion, therefore, leads you to that vocation where you can have maximum impact and influence.

The reason people huddle around a campfire at night is the same reason people are drawn to people with passion—your passion is a source of light, warmth, and hope. So don't get too hung up on what you do. Focus on your passion, because that's where the light and the warmth is—your impact and influence.

Yet, sometimes identifying your true passion is as difficult as identifying your talent. Your talent isn't necessarily your passion, and vice versa. For instance, you might have a talent for playing the piano or guitar, but it might not be your passion, it might not be the thing that drives you to excel. You might be aware of your innate talent and have identified the gift you were born with, but sometimes you're numbed to your passion and find it difficult to feel. Sometimes you're deaf to its whispers and cannot hear its call.

Not to worry, there are three tests you can easily perform to rediscover your passion. They are: The Deathbed Test, The Lotto Test, and The Mirror Test.

#1: The Deathbed Test

This test is a thought experiment in which you imagine your last day here on earth. It may sound morbid, but it's an extremely effective tool to cut through all the mental barriers preventing you from connecting with your real passion. It requires you to be honest with yourself and putting aside your fears of death. But if thinking about your death is too uncomfortable, move on to the next test.

If you're okay with it, find a place where you won't be disturbed for half an hour. Then begin the test by closing your eyes and imagining yourself on your deathbed surrounded by loved ones.

Imagine this moment in as much detail as you can. When do you think this will happen? How old will you be? Who is at your bedside? Your partner, children, grandchildren, other family members, good friends? There may be candles and incense. What do you see outside the window? Note the colour of the walls and the silence. Or is there music playing? What do the sheets feel like, the blankets? Are you hot or cold?

Once you are comfortable with the setting, imagine that time is ending. Imagine you have only five breaths left before you pass on. What do you feel? What emotions are you feeling?

There may be disappointments, regrets, feelings of anger, injustice, hatred, fear. These feelings are entirely normal in the circumstance. Don't push them away. Don't ignore them, no matter how uncomfortable they feel. The discomfort won't last. These feelings have a message for you, so try to understand what that message is.

Ask your future self, the self that is lying on your deathbed, 'Why am I feeling this way? What is the lesson I need to learn?'

When performed properly, the Deathbed Test will reveal your true passion. It will invariably be found through your biggest regret.

#2: The Lotto Test

Although money is an important aspect of life, the desire for it can sometimes cloud your vision of who you really are. Worse, it can prevent you from discovering your true calling and vocation. The Lotto Test bypasses the obstacles that the need for money puts in your path and clears the way to finding your passion.

The Lotto Test is simply this: Imagine that you've won a billion dollars in the world's richest lottery. What do you do now?

I assume you'll have one heck of a party. You'll travel the world. You'll buy huge mansions, luxury cars, designer clothes, expensive jewellery. You'll buy all the things that money can buy, all the things you've ever dreamed of having. Because now you can.

But now I want you to project yourself four or five years down the track, after you've worn yourself out traveling and shopping, after you can't bear the thought of another glass of champagne or celebrity party. What do you do now?

What do you do now that you've got it all and done it all? What is it you really want now that money is no obstacle? Is there something more you want to achieve? What do you dream of doing? Is there something you want to do for the rest of your life without wanting to retire from it?

I'm sure there is. I'm sure there's some burning passion inside you just waiting for your attention. I'm sure there's more to your life than having everything you could ever want. What is it for you? What is that thing that money can't buy?

Find the answer to that and you find your passion.

#3: The Mirror Test

The Deathbed Test asks you to project yourself into the future and look back over your life to examine how you wish it had transpired. It gives you the power of hindsight before it's happened. It gives you the chance to see how the choices you make today affect your future.

The Lotto Test asks you to imagine that money is no obstacle, that you can no longer use the excuse of paying the bills to justify not following your passion, to not listening to your calling. With all the funds at your disposal, it reveals what dreams you want to make real. It reveals what life you want to build, to create, to manifest.

The Mirror Test does not ask you to imagine anything, either now or in the future. It simply instructs you to stand in front of the bathroom mirror when you get out of bed, look yourself in the eye, and ask yourself this question:

Am I doing all I can today to live my passion?

IT'S UP TO YOU!

Listen to the answer your reflection gives you, not the excuses, and you'll find your passion.

I—INTELLECT

Your intellect is spectrum of awareness and perception. It is your capacity to receive and interpret information, a measure of your ability to perceive reality as it truly is. Think of your intellect as your own Central Intelligence Agency (CIA), which 'Captures' information, 'Interprets' or translates that information, and becomes 'Aware' of that information and its significance.

Take vision, for example. Your eyes are visual organs that receive and transmit colours, shapes, and movements of the outside world via electrochemical impulses to your brain's visual cortex where they are translated as images and observations by your consciousness. Without your eyes capturing visual stimuli and a consciousness to interpret them, you can't see. Both the organ (eye) and the interpreting consciousness constitute the 'visual' intellect.

You also have more than one type of intellect. You in fact have four types, which encompass all aspects of your being: mental, emotional, physical, and spiritual. These are the four 'eyes' or organs of your CIA that you use to 'see' with. Without these organs of perception, you cannot observe yourself, your environment, or the interaction of yourself with your environment.

There are levels of intellect too. There are levels of intellect between species, and there are levels within species. Humans, for instance, have the highest intellect of all the known species on earth. A dolphin is more intelligent than a dog, but dogs are more intelligent than cats or birds. Some people are also smarter than others. Some dogs are smarter than others.

There are also levels within the different types of intellect. Just as vision is a spectrum, with blindness at the lower end and 20/20 vision at the highest end, and degrees of short- and long-sightedness in the middle, your four intellects also sit within a spectrum.

The higher your intellect, the greater your capacity to 'see', the more information you are able to capture, interpret, and observe. The more you can perceive, the more you are 'aware'. Just like climbing a mountain, the higher you ascend, the further you can see. Genius, for instance, is the mastery of human intellect, and it comes in all shapes and sizes. A genius intellect resides at the peak of the intellectual mountain and can 'see' further than those not as high on the mountain. Einstein was a mental genius. Michael Jordan was a physical genius. Gandhi was an emotional (moral/ethical) genius. Rumi was a spiritual genius.

You may not be on the same level as genius, but you certainly have an intellectual capability that encompasses your mental, emotional, physical, and spiritual being. That's because your intellect is inherent; you were born with it.

It just needs the time and proper nurturing to mature.

Mental Intellect (IQ)

When you think, you think with your mind, the organ of mental intellect, which is most often associated with your Intelligence Quotient (IQ).[34] As the 'eye' of mental awareness and perception, your mind 'sees' mental imagery and information through thought processing. Your IQ is your capacity to perceive ideas, dreams, memories, concepts, and beliefs.

But your mental intellect is more than just an IQ score. *You* are more than just an IQ score. You're bigger than that. Your ability to problem solve and adapt to changing circumstances is one of your biggest and best attributes. Your logical left brain and creative right brain can shape your mental capabilities into many forms:

---

[34] An IQ is a score totalled from a series of standardised tests aimed at assessing an individual's mental intelligence. The median IQ score is 100, with two-thirds of the population between 85 and 115. Genius is considered above 140.

IT'S UP TO YOU!

- Numeracy and mathematics.
- Literacy and reading.
- Language and communication.
- Science and health.
- Art and music.
- Religion and metaphysics.
- Psychology and emotions/feelings.

Take a moment to consider your natural inclinations. What books or magazines do you read for pleasure? What subjects engross you? What courses or topics have you found the most enjoyable? If you have a hobby or play a musical instrument, what is the most intellectually stimulating aspect of it?

Remember, though, your IQ is just one part of your overall intellect. But understanding your unique mental intellect is a great exercise to get direction and navigate your way to your niche.

Emotional Intellect (EQ)

In Chapter 2 we discussed how some psychologists define emotions as physical responses to stimuli, such as stress, and define feelings as psychological responses to stimuli, such as fear and worry. For our purposes, however, we will consider that when you feel an emotion, you feel it in your heart.

Your heart was the very first organ to develop just six weeks after you were conceived, developing in utero much earlier than your brain. When seen via ultrasound, a heartbeat is considered the first sign of life of a foetus. It even has its own neural network that can 'think' for itself without instruction from the brain, which is why your heart is the organ of your emotional intellect (EQ).[35]

---

[35] Although not without its critics, the term 'Emotional Quotient' (EQ) or Emotional Intelligence (EI) has gained popular appeal since 1995 with the release of the bestselling book, *Emotional Intelligence*, by Daniel Goleman.

BROWN DIAMOND: FIND YOUR NICHE

As the 'eye' of emotional awareness and perception, your heart 'sees' emotional imagery and information through feelings. Your EQ is your capacity to sense love, anger, fear, hatred, happiness, as well as your ability to empathise with others.

Your EQ affects the way you interact with others, your family, partner, community, work colleagues, even the way you interact with animals and nature. It affects your ability to accurately perceive and understand yours and other's emotions, as well as adjusting and expressing your emotions appropriately.

Whereby your IQ is mostly fixed and unchangeable, your EQ isn't. You can raise your EQ with compassion, love, awareness, and other mindfulness techniques to scale the EQ mountain. The more you are in touch with your feelings, the more you can use your emotions to positively enhance your thought processes and behaviours. These qualities are most noticeable in those who have taken time to develop and mature the organ of their emotional intellect—their heart.

The flipside of these qualities is that of an immature emotional intellect, and below is a table of qualities of those with high EQ and low EQ:

HIGH EQ	LOW EQ
Ability to delay gratification	Uncaring and intolerance of others
Respect for truth and justice	Disrespect of the law
Tolerance and acceptance of others	Dishonesty and disloyalty
Integrity and self-worth	Impatience and quickness to anger
Values and morals	Selfishness and entitlement

TABLE 14:   High EQ Vs Low EQ

IT'S UP TO YOU!

Your EQ is an important determinant in your personal brand of success. Therefore, take the time to know and understand your EQ.

Kinaesthetic Intelligence and Physical Intellect (PQ)

Your physical body is the result of your genetic code, and your body is the organ of your physical intellect (PQ). As the 'eye' of physical awareness and perception, your body 'sees' physical imagery and information through your five senses of sight, sound, touch, taste, and smell. Your PQ is your capacity to feel pleasure and pain, bodily energy, and cyclic rhythms.

Our physical prowess, however, is not as important as our mental prowess. In terms of physical attributes, humans are quite weak and vulnerable. Nevertheless, one physical attribute stands us out in the animal kingdom—our ability to run long distances.

Humans have great stamina. We are built to run. Although physically weaker and slower than many species, we can outlast most animals in terms of distance. In the past, one of the tactics used by our hunter-gatherer ancestors was to relentlessly chase a prey, like a deer, until it fell into exhaustion. The animal would collapse without a fight, leaving the hunter to deliver the fatal blow. It sometimes took 24 hours to run them down, but our innate endurance meant that our ancestors could hunt prey without risking life and limb in a potentially fatal encounter.

Endurance, though, is just one example of physical intellect:

PHYSICAL INTELLECT (PQ)	
Athleticism and coordination	'Gut feelings' and instincts
Dexterity and flexibility	Natural cycles and rhythms
Balance and poise	Self-healing and immunity
Alertness and reactivity	Muscle memory and endurance

TABLE 15: Physical Intellect (PQ)

BROWN DIAMOND: FIND YOUR NICHE

Michael Jordan, Ayrton Senna, Jack Nicklaus, and Margaret Court were sportsmen and women at the peak of human physical intellect. You may not be at that elite level, or even fully abled, it doesn't matter. What matters is that you take a moment to consider the activities you're drawn to, such as running, cycling, gymnastics, swimming, and other sports. Consider also what hobbies or professional industries interest you, such as physiotherapy and massage, dancing and gymnastics, carpentry and sculpting, personal training and sports coaching, gardening and agriculture, and so forth.

Understanding your own physical intellect helps you to understand your own unique abilities and capabilities. Remember though, your physical intellect is more than just your ability to run long distances or jump high. For instance, your natural cycles and gut feelings. In today's 24-hour society, our body's rhythms and cycles have changed from what they were two hundred years ago before electricity kept the lights burning all night. Your personal sleeping cycles are part of your physical intellect, but if you're not 'in sync' with them you can experience insomnia, increasing tiredness, and all the negative side-effects that sleep deprivation has on your mental status.

Your gut feelings and instincts are also important. Are you comfortable with them, or do you dismiss them as irrelevant and emotional?

There are many more aspects to the human physical intellect. Suffice to say, getting in tune with your own innate abilities and capabilities puts you in a better position to know your thing and find your niche.

Spiritual Intellect (SQ)

Your human spirit, or soul, is the organ of your spiritual intellect

(SQ).[36] As the 'eye' of your spiritual awareness and perception, your soul 'sees' spiritual imagery and information through intuition and insight. Your SQ is your capacity to see the unseen order of things, the interconnectedness that unites the entire universe. To feel the stillness from which all energy emanates, to sense eternity in this moment of now.

Of the four intellects, nothing distinguishes humans from other animals more than our spiritual intelligence, even more than our mental intelligence. Only humans can observe the non-material and non-temporal aspects of themselves and their environment. This is because only humans have a spiritual intellect that can observe who we are *prior* to space and time. Only humans can observe that which is beyond the capabilities of scientific instrumentation. Only we can see our true self.

Despite its transcendent and abstract nature, your spiritual intellect is the glue that binds your mental, emotional, and physical intellects together. Below is a diagram of how your four intelligences are connected and balanced in a single, united awareness:

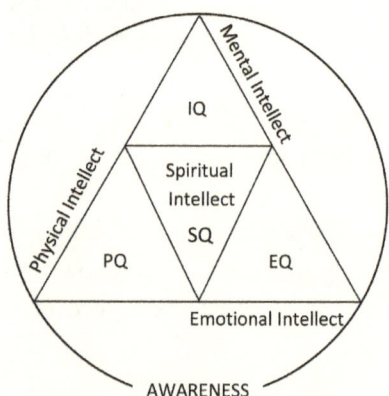

FIGURE 18:   Human Intellect—Mental, Emotional, Physical, Spiritual

---

[36] Spirituality is not religiosity, although religion falls under its umbrella.

BROWN DIAMOND: FIND YOUR NICHE

Yet, the organ of spiritual intellect—your soul—is perhaps the most underused and ignored of all the four 'eyes'. Like the four legs of a chair, if one leg is broken or cut, it's very difficult to sit without unbalancing and tipping over. Likewise, the fullness of life can only be seen and experienced when all four intelligences are balanced in harmony with one another. That includes your spiritual intellect.

You already have it, so don't waste it. Put it to good use and maximise your potential as a human being. As some have claimed, you are not a human being having a spiritual experience, you are a spiritual being having a human experience.

N—NATURE & PERSONALITY

The American Psychological Association (APA) defines personality as the 'individual differences in characteristic patterns of thinking, feeling, and behaving.' Our personality is important to who we are—our identity—and strongly correlates with overall life satisfaction.[37]

Essentially, your personality is the creation of your four intellects: what you think of yourself, what you feel of yourself, what you experience of yourself, and what you believe of yourself. Every mother knows their child is born with a distinct personality. No two babies are the same, even twins. As a human being, your innate disposition is developed and matured as you grow into adulthood. Your adult personality is therefore a result of your genetics and your environment, of both nature and nurture.

Your personality, though, isn't your character. Your character is aligned with your spiritual intelligence, whereas your personality is more closely aligned with your ego—your likes and dislikes, your wants and desires, your emotions and reactions—which is

---

[37] Boyce CJ, Wood AM, Powdthavee N, *Is Personality Fixed? Personality changes as much as 'variable' economic factors and more strongly predicts changes to life satisfaction*, Social Indicators Research, 2013.

therefore more influenced by your mental, emotional, and physical intellects.

Below is a diagram of how your character and personality are balanced with your four intellects:

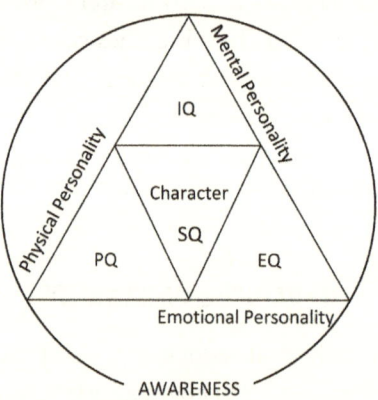

FIGURE 19: Character and Personality

Your IQ contributes to your mental personality, such as your logic, language, learning, and imagination. Your EQ contributes to your emotional personality, such as your interests, empathy, relationships, and predominant emotions (e.g. fear, anger, desire, hatred). Your PQ contributes to your physical personality, such as your physical appearance (eye colour, height, sex), as well as your athletic ability, dexterity, and instincts. Your spiritual intellect contributes to your spiritual personality, your character, which we have discussed previously.

Human personality is a complex issue. It's been the subject of research since the time of Plato and Aristotle, and more recently by the likes of Freud, Jung, Maslow, and Goldberg. The latter is credited with identifying the 'Big Five' personality factors, the most current theory to date on human personality.[38]

---

[38] The Big Five normative test does have its critics as a model to accurately measure personality traits because of its behaviour-based method of research. Other personality predictor models include the Personality Based Recommender

The Big Five are known collectively as OCEAN: Openness to Experience, Conscientiousness, Extroversion, Agreeableness, and Neuroticism.

Openness to Experience

The willingness to experience novelty, to accept vulnerability, and to think laterally. People with high openness to experience are more likely to hold liberal or progressive views over and above traditional views. They are charismatic, artistic, and adventurous. They also show creative leadership qualities and tend to promote peace and tolerance of others.

Although this factor is the least likely of the Big Five factors to change over time, it is the most likely factor to help you learn and grow. The table below highlights personality traits associated with high openness to experience and with low openness to experience.

HIGH OPENNESS TO EXPERIENCE	LOW OPENNESS TO EXPERIENCE
Daring and curiosity	Routine and procedure
Creativeness and originality	Adherence to rules
Intellectuality and contemplativeness	Technical thinking
Imagination and insightfulness	Low tolerance for risk
Interests in things and people	Minimal social interaction

TABLE 16: Openness to Experience

Systems and Cattell's 16 Personality Factor (16PF) test. Nonetheless, the Big Five personality factors are sufficient for our purposes, which is to help you identify your nature and personality.

Conscientiousness

The inclination toward social acceptability, emotional control, and goal-directed activity. People with high conscientiousness are usually successful in their chosen field. They make great managers, schoolteachers, nurses, defence force and police officers, along with any other profession that involves planning and organising, duty, and sticking to procedures. They are able to delay gratification and are naturally drawn to conformity and security.

The table below highlights personality traits associated with high and low conscientiousness.

HIGH CONSCIENTIOUSNESS	LOW CONSCIENTIOUSNESS
Self-discipline and thoroughness	Impulsive and impatient
Predictability and reliability	Laid back and blasé
Vigilance and carefulness	Non-committal
Resourcefulness and high work ethic	Lacking focus and unreliable
Persistence and perseverance	Low work ethic

TABLE 17:   Conscientiousness

Extroversion

This factor also includes its opposite, which is introversion. The extroversion personality factor is more of a spectrum, with extroverts talking loudly in one corner of the party, introverts sitting alone in the other corner, and everyone else in between.

Extroverts tend to need and seek out the attention of others. They draw their energy from other people and prefer group activities over doing things on their own. They may also like to socialise with many people and have a large network of friends.

At the other end of the spectrum, introverts are more comfortable being alone and tend to avoid others if they can. They draw their energy from within themselves, and prefer a selection of few, close friends over a large network of friends. They enjoy engaging in quieter, more peaceful activities than with a larger group of people.

The table below highlights personality traits associated with extroversion and introversion.

EXTROVERSION	INTROVERSION
Assertiveness and activeness	Introspection and quietude
Excitement and pleasure seeking	Reservedness and shyness
Sociability and friendliness	Thoughtfulness and considerateness
Expressiveness and affection	Cautiousness and prudence

TABLE 18:   Extroversion

Agreeableness

As the name suggests, agreeableness regards how well you interact and get along with others. How likeable you are, in other words. Those high with agreeableness are not only well-liked, but they are respected and appreciated. They are sympathetic and sensitive toward others, even strangers, and show affection to close friends and family. Those with low agreeableness traits are less well-liked and have low trustworthiness.

The table below highlights personality traits associated with high agreeableness and low agreeableness.

HIGH AGREEABLENESS	LOW AGREEABLENESS
Humility and modesty	Rudeness and off-handedness
Amiability and cheerfulness	Antagonism and callousness
Politeness and tactfulness	Intolerance and irritation
Loyalty and unselfishness	Disloyalty and selfishness
Patience and helpfulness	Sarcasm and facetiousness

TABLE 19: Agreeableness

Neuroticism (emotional stability)

This factor differs from the previous factors in that it emphasises the negative end of the scale. So those with high neuroticism have low emotional stability. They may be quick to anger and get moody. They also have low self-esteem, are overly self-conscious and unsure of themselves.

Those with low neuroticism are more self-confident and adventurous. They also have higher self-esteem, are surer of themselves, and don't allow negative self-doubt or worry get the better of them.

The table below highlights personality traits associated with high neuroticism and low neuroticism

HIGH NEUROTICISM	LOW NEUROTICISM
Anxiousness and fearfulness	Calmness and composure
Insecurity and oversensitivity	Self-assurance and self-reliance
Hedonism and impulsiveness	Optimism and resilience
Low self-confidence and high self-criticism	Life-skills and coping ability

TABLE 20: Neuroticism

BROWN DIAMOND: FIND YOUR NICHE

G—GENERAL EXPERIENCE

Your general experience is the one facet of your THING that is most adaptable and open to change through your Life Leadership journey.

No one else has your unique experiences in life. Your experiences have played a role in how you think and how you behave. They have helped shape who you are, and they have influenced the choice of career you've made, the relationships you've developed, and the beliefs you adhere to.

Sociologists claim that the current generation of school leavers will have five to seven different careers in their lifetime. Gone are the days of 'a job for life'. Not counting my university days, I myself have had five careers to date: doctor, author, publisher, digital marketer, and professional speaker. This doesn't include the coaching and mentoring I do, so it could realistically count as seven different careers.

I consider all my careers, as diverse as they are, as building my skills and experience to fulfil my life purpose as a Life Leader—which is to help you find your purpose and direction in life.

What is your general experience, and what is the underlying thread tying all your experiences together?

You will find that your THING is always evolving as you pass through your life stages. As diamonds are found rough and in need of polishing, so too your THING needs constant polishing.

My THING is no different. It is always evolving and adapting, and it's something I'll share it with you now with the intent to help you develop and polish yours:

> *Talent*: I have a talent for storytelling and 'reading' people's true nature and intent.
>
> *Heart*: My passion is writing, personal development, and helping others fulfil their potential.

Intellect: My mental intellect is conceptual. My emotional intellect is empathic. My physical intellect is presence. My spiritual intellect is awareness.

Nature: My personality is contemplative and leans towards introversion.

General Experience: doctor, author, writer, publisher, speaker, mentor, coach, father, brother, son, husband, friend, traveller, sport addict, volunteer, and very average soccer player.

My THING points me in the direction of my niche, that place where I was born to be and where I can have most impact and influence for the good of others. It's that place where I want to be, where I *know* I should be.

You too can find your special place in this world. Your THING will help you do it.

Once you know your THING, another good exercise is to extrapolate it to the future by imagining being the best at what you do.

-> How far can your *talent* take you? How can you master your skillset?

-> How can you turn your *passion* into a reality?

-> Where do your *four intellects* direct you?

-> What natural path does your *personality* take you?

-> Where does your *general experience* lead next?

Write your answers down and review them regularly. They will remind you of the vision of who you are growing into and the place where you want to be—your *niche*.

BROWN DIAMOND PRACTICE—REALIGN WITH YOUR NICHE

The exercise for brown diamond level is to realign yourself with your niche. Doing so will help you to stay on track and keep moving toward the vision you have of who you want to be and what you want to do.

The acronym REALIGNED is a great way to accomplish this:

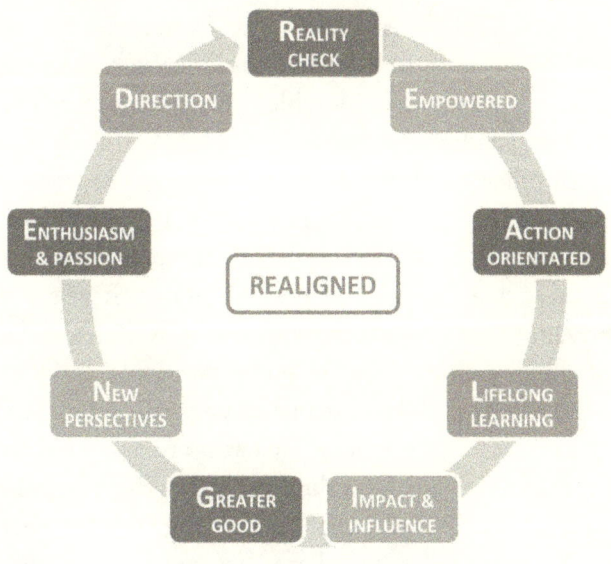

FIGURE 20:   Realigned

R: Reality Check

The first thing to consider whether you are realigned with your niche is a reality check. How deep does your passion feel? Is your niche pie in the sky stuff, just a dream, or is it something that is ingrained in every fibre of your body? Do you feel you have a special place you were born for?

The depth to which you are committed to finding your niche is proportional to the successful achievement of it. If your niche isn't something you believe you can make real, you won't be committed to it and you'll most likely give up at the first hurdle.

Your 'reality check' question to realign yourself is:

Is my niche worth the time and effort to attain it?

E: Empowered

Knowing your THING is empowering. When you are realigned with your niche, *you* are empowering. You achieve things you previously considered unachievable. You develop presence. You become a Life Leader.

One summer in Interlaken, Switzerland, I went up the mountains and hiked through the meadows. When I sat down for a rest and contemplated the ice-capped giants around me, I suddenly had the sense that I could feel the mountains. It was a massive, heavy presence that coursed through my body. A sense that these mountains were not just gigantic, but *immoveable*.

This is the same feeling you get when you are realigned with your niche, that you are immoveable, that you are anchored to where you are meant to be. You have the feeling that there is nothing else in this world that you are meant to be doing. You feel that this is who you are meant to be and what you were born to become. This feeling is unshakeable. It is *empowering*.

It's the feeling of a giant.

But if you currently feel disempowered, you will do well to stand back and question whether you've fallen off track or whether you're on the wrong track all together.

Your 'empowerment' question to realign yourself is:

Does my niche make me feel empowered or disempowered?

A: Action Orientated

Your niche is that place where you manifest your dreams and intentions. But only through action can your intentions be turned into something real and tangible.

In this Game of Life in which we play out the game of giving and receiving, the emphasis is on the verb 'play', which is action. You must give to receive, and receive to give. Through action you give, and through action you receive.

Action is how you receive what you want. Sitting back and waiting for the world to serve you isn't how the game works. You could be waiting an awfully long time. Winners win the game by being pro-active. They win the game by serving others. They win the game by going out there and getting things done.

Your 'action orientated' question to realign yourself is:

Does my niche motivate me to action?

L: Lifelong Learning

Lifelong learning is a bit of a misnomer because life is a full-time education. But not every student becomes a master of what they do or wants to. Not every writer wants to become a raconteur. Not every musician wants to become a maestro. Not everyone sets out to achieve mastery.

But Life Leaders do. They know that mastery is the process with which they can become who they want to be and achieve what they want to achieve. This requires a passion for learning, to be better today than yesterday, to reach a level of understanding that transcends to mastery.

Then they keep going. They keep learning. Because once they achieve mastery, a whole new world opens that had remained closed right up until that moment.

Just as a view remains unseen until you have climbed to the peak of the mountain.

Your 'lifelong learning' question to realign yourself is:

Will my niche lead me to mastery?

I: Impact & Influence

You know when you are aligned with your niche because your sphere of influence grows. You start to get known for knowing something. You start to have voice. People listen to what you have to say. They take on board the advice and teaching you have to offer. You begin to have meaningful impact on people's lives.

This is the value you bring to the table. You are a person of values, and you are a person of value. People want to know you because they value who you are and what you can do for them.

You are a person of worth, a Life Leader.

Your 'impact and influence' question to realign yourself is:

What value does my niche bring to the table?

G: Greater Good

As with your impact and influence, another indicator of whether you are aligned with your niche is how much you are dedicated to the greater good. You are no longer just interested in your own wellbeing, but the wellbeing of others—your family, friends, community, country, the world. It's the difference between having a short-sighted, self-centred goal and a longsighted, world centric vision.

It's a cliché, but people don't care about how much you know until they know how much you care. Life Leaders care about others. They care about working for a higher purpose and a worthy cause.

They care about making the world a better place.

Your 'greater good' question to realign yourself is:

Does my niche work for me and for others?

N: New Perspectives

People who are stuck in a rut feel as if nothing is going to change. Worse, they feel as if the whole world is conspiring against them and preventing them from doing what they really want to do. They can't see a way out. They are blind to the opportunities that life offers them.

The contemporary definition of insanity is to do the same thing over and over again and expect a different result. Life Leaders know this, which is why they look for new ways of thinking... and find them. In fact, they find so many new perspectives they have to pick and choose which ones they want to invest themselves in. Because when you start seeing the bigger picture of life, life presents itself as a smorgasbord of choice, always new and fresh.

When you are realigned with your niche, new perspectives are a way of life, new opportunities present themselves every day.

Your 'new perspectives' question to realign yourself is:

Does my niche let me see the bigger picture?

E: Enthusiasm & Passion

As we discussed, passion is what your purpose feels like. But if passion is an ocean, then enthusiasm is the waves you see above the waterline. To be enthusiastic is to be momentarily filled with vibrancy, to be filled with the energy of life. It is the short-lived spurt of energy that swells from the depths of passion.

Take note of your enthusiasm, then, because it points to what lies deeper within. Use it to dive into your passion and stay aligned with your niche.

Your 'enthusiasm and passion' question to realign yourself is:

Does my niche ignite the fire in me?

D: Direction

Your niche is not only an empowering force, but it is also a magnetic force—a force of attraction. No matter where in the world you are, a compass will always align with the earth's magnetic field and point north. It's a navigational tool. Your niche is just like the magnetic north pole: it's your direction finder.

Wherever you are in your journey, you can always realign with your niche and always be sure to navigate in the right direction—to where you were born to be.

Your 'direction' question to realign yourself is:

Does my niche give me direction and keep me on track?

10 YELLOW DIAMOND: POWER UP YOUR BELIEFS

LIFE LEADERSHIP PRACTICE #3

THE NEXT LEVEL of your Life Leadership journey is yellow diamond. The aim of this level is to attain focus-level knowledge of Life Skill #4–How, and progress to blue diamond level within 3-4 months. The practice of powering up your beliefs is the first in the process of 'Rejuvenating' and moving into Quadrant #1 in the Empowered Living Index.

The core of this Life Leadership Practice is to understand how behaviours and habits of success are strongly influenced by your thoughts and beliefs. In The Diamond Triangle, your beliefs form the first of three building blocks in your 'I Can' axis, and is now looking like this:

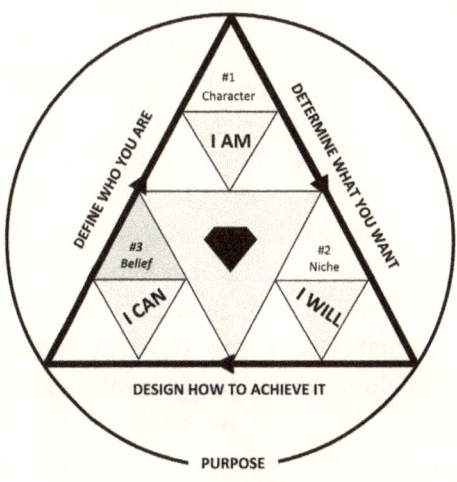

FIGURE 21:   Yellow Diamond—Belief

IT'S UP TO YOU!

MIND YOUR MOTTO

You can't live a positive life with a negative mindset, as the bumper sticker says.

The way you perceive the world, the filters through which you see life around you, the belief systems that you adhere to, are key to how you experience yourself and your life-situation. For instance, those who claim to be realists are just socially acceptable pessimists. But where a pessimist sees a problem in every opportunity, an optimist sees an opportunity in every problem. Your beliefs are essential to how far you achieve your own personal brand of success, and how close you get to fulfilling your potential and living the life you deserve.

Whether you are aware of it or not, your core beliefs have a huge influence over your life. They are the set guidelines you use, either consciously or unconsciously, to determine your thoughts, emotions, and actions. They are a double-edged sword, however, because they can either empower you to success or disempower you through self-sabotage.

As a Life Leader, you need to identify the beliefs that are holding you back and limiting your success. Your beliefs determine your perception of life and therefore your experience of life. If you fail to analyse the thoughts and beliefs you hold about yourself, others, and the world, you'll be destined to experience your past again and again until those thoughts and beliefs change. That's why it's been said that you can't solve your problems with the same level of thinking that created them.

Beliefs are the truths you accept, whether they are supported by facts or not. Like all thoughts, they can be conscious or unconscious. Conscious beliefs are the easiest to change because they are most obvious and apparent to you. However, it's the unconscious beliefs, the hidden ones, that are difficult to root out because you're not aware of them, nor are you aware of their power over you.

YELLOW DIAMOND: POWER UP YOUR BELIEFS

But you don't need to dig too deep to find them. Your mottos are a great pointer to the beliefs, attitudes, and values you hold close to your heart. A lot of people don't realise they subscribe to a motto, but everyone has them. They are the bumper stickers we wear on our backside.

Here are some common mottos that people say:

MOTTOS	
Life's a jungle; only the fittest survive.	Money doesn't grow on trees.
Do unto others before they do unto you.	The end justifies the means.
Money makes the world go 'round.	You need money to make money.
All men are the same.	It's a man's world.
All women are the same.	There's no such thing as miracles.

TABLE 21: Mottos

Mottos are taglines of your underlying belief system, and therefore your experience. Tell yourself one hundred times a day that all women are the same, and guess what your experience of women will be? Tell yourself thousands of times that life's a jungle, that it's everyone for themselves, women and children included, and guess what your experience of life will be?

Some women have suffered heartache and terrible abuse from men, but does that make all men the same? Some men have suffered as the result of somebody else's dishonesty, but does that mean everyone in the world wants to exploit them? Does the end justify the means, especially when there are no ends in life, only means?

Your mottos and attitudes are extremely important because

how you think is how you feel is how you act. Your thought processes determine your behaviour. Negative thought processes lead to negative, self-limiting and self-sabotaging behaviours. Positive thought processes lead to positive, non-limiting and self-empowering behaviours.

Take a moment to consider the mottos you subscribe to, then ask yourself if they influence the way you speak to yourself and others, and whether they also influence your behaviours. Consider also whether these mottos are actually true, and if not, whether changing them in a positive way could help change your life-situation in a positive way.

Here are a few life affirming mottos from some of history's most influential people:

> *You either believe miracles happen every day, or not at all.*
> ~ Albert Einstein.

> *Believe you can and you're halfway there.*
> ~ Theodore Roosevelt

> *Nothing is impossible, the word itself says, 'I'm possible!'*
> ~ Audrey Hepburn

> *Man is where he is so that he may learn that he may grow.*
> ~ James Allen

> *Gratitude is the single most important ingredient to living a successful and fulfilled life.*
> ~ Jack Canfield

> *Act as if what you do makes a difference. It does.*
> ~ William James

REPETITIVE THOUGHTS

Your head is the gymnasium of the mind. You can either use it regularly and build up a strong, fit, and healthy mind, or you can ignore it and let your mind atrophy through inaction. Positive thoughts build mental strength. Repeat them regularly in a mental workout and the mind gets stronger.

Researchers estimate that of the 12,000 to 60,000 thoughts we have every day, 90-98% are repetitive. That means more than 9 out of 10 thoughts you've had today are replays of what you thought yesterday. You are constantly watching the same program over and over again on the TV screen of your mind. Worse, 80% of those thoughts are negative.

This equates to an astonishing *3 to 7 million negative thoughts* per person per year.

Imagine, though, if every human being on the planet could flip their thinking into 3 to 7 million positive thoughts per year? Imagine what a wonderful world we would create.

But that is only half the battle. Our brains are seemingly wired to catch negative thoughts and let positive thoughts slide. It's as if the human brain has evolved sticky and slippery neurones. The sticky neurones clump negative thoughts together, and the slippery neurones to let positive thoughts slide right by. What we have is a brain made of 80% sticky and 20% slippery neurones. Somehow, we have to train our brain into catching 80% positive thoughts and letting the negative thoughts slide.

This is not as hard as it seems. Scientists have discovered that repetitive thoughts affect the physical pathways in the brain. Your neural pathways are not set in stone. Your brain is not marble; it is a malleable and flexible organ that can adapt to its circumstances. For instance, stroke victims can be taught to speak or walk again after the part of the brain controlling those functions has died or been damaged. Through repetitive rehabilitation, the brain of the stroke victim can be rewired to control movement and balance, even speech. Of course, it depends on the size of the stroke and the affected area of the brain, but new neural pathways can be formed to bypass the affected area and allow the once disabled stroke victim to walk and talk again.

IT'S UP TO YOU!

Although this is great news for stroke victims, it's also great news for everybody. You can rewire your brain through repetitive action. You do this anyhow, only you probably do it subconsciously. You can actively and consciously rewire your brain how you want it to be rewired. You can do this through repetitive *intentional* thoughts of who you want to be, what you want to achieve, and how you can achieve it.

The city of Adelaide in South Australia is bordered by sea to the west and hills to the east. In the mid-19th Century, engineers were laying the railway line between Adelaide and Melbourne, Victoria, and were confronted with the challenge of planning a route up and over the Adelaide Hills. They couldn't go straight up because steam engines at the time were not powerful enough to haul the carriages in a direct line over the hills. They needed to find a route with the least amount of incline.

To overcome this problem, they happened upon a clever solution. Feral goats had been allowed to roam the area for decades, leaving trails up and down the faces of the hills. Goats instinctively know the easiest route up an incline. Just as water takes the route of least resistance as it flows down towards the sea, so too goats follow lines of least resistance up a hill or mountain. The answer was to build the railway following the meandering goat trails up the hills, and those same railway lines are still in use today.

The goat trails were formed by thousands and thousands of hooves traveling over the same ground, creating ruts in the earth. Over time, the goats just followed where other goats had gone before them. They didn't even have to think of the easiest way up the hill; it had already been done. So too the engineers laying the railway line. They didn't have to work out the best way up the hills; the goats had already done it for them.

The same process works in the brain. When thousands and thousands, even millions, of thoughts pass through the same pathways of the brain, mental paths or 'ruts' are carved by these thoughts forming channels or trails of least resistance. This is the reason most of our thoughts are made without much consideration. It's easier. Our thoughts follow the path of least resistance. For most of the time they just appear, travel along the same neural pathway millions of thoughts have previously gone, and then disappear, followed by another, then another, then another. This is why 90-98% of your thoughts are repetitive.

The science behind this is called myelination. Your neurones or braincells are connected to each other through wire-like extensions called axons, and there are billions of these connections in your brain. An axon meets another neurone's dendrite at a junction called a synapse. Communication between neurones occurs through chemical electro-charges, which pass from one neurone to another down the axon and across the synapse.

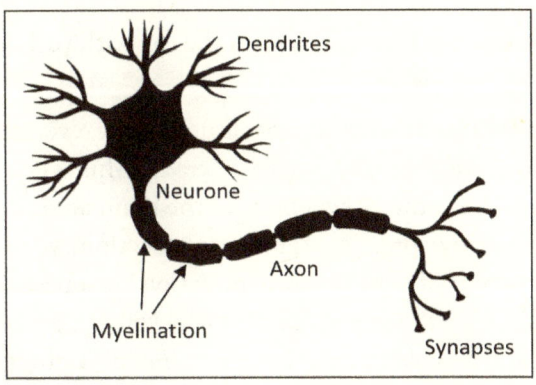

FIGURE 22:   Neurone & Myelinated Axon

The speed at which that chemical electro-charge passes down the axon is dependent on how thick the axon is. The thicker the axon, the quicker it sends its signals, the quicker you think. The axon is thickened in an insulation process called myelination, and this gives the brain its white colour. Other braincells called oligodendrocytes insulate the axons by wrapping them in sheaths of myelin. If you were to take a cross-section of a myelinated axon, it would look like rings of tree. The more 'rings' the axon has, the quicker its electro-charge can travel to the next neurone.

When Einstein died, his autopsy discovered that his brain was almost pure white. This was because it was significantly more myelinated than the average human brain. It's estimated that he could think 100x faster than most people, which made him a genius.

No matter your age, new connections are happening all the time in your brain. Axons are meeting other neurones whenever you perform a new task. This is how your brain rewires itself after a stroke. Try this quick exercise to prove this to yourself:

-> Sit down in a chair and get yourself comfortable.

-> Stretch your right leg out and turn your right foot in a clockwise direction.

-> Now draw a number 6 from the top with your index finger in the air.

You can't do it. Either your foot automatically reverses in an anti-clockwise direction, or you draw a reverse 6. This is because this is a new exercise and the connections in the brain aren't myelinated. But with repetitive practice, the new connections you've made in the brain become myelinated and the action becomes 'fixed'.

Myelination is the science behind why you can get on a bicycle after years and be able to balance almost immediately. It's also why bad habits are so hard to break.

But it's also the science of how you create new habits of success.

CHANGING YOUR THOUGHTS

The rewiring of your brain means that new habits can be created very quickly, and you can enact change within minutes. But if the new axons/connections aren't myelinated with deliberate intent (e.g. actions, behaviours, thoughts, affirmations) over a period of time, then the new change will not be permanent. This is why it can take 21 days for a new habit to become set, such as changing diets, going to the gym, saving money, and other new habits you want.

But it also means changing your way of thinking is difficult. You can't teach an old dog new tricks, and a leopard can't change its spots, or so they say. Once your thought patterns are set, once your neural pathways have been carved through your brain, much of your thought content is just a repetition of what you've always thought. Even though your brain is malleable, the flow of identical thought processes for years and years creates deep mental ruts and channels that are seemingly set like concrete troughs. You know when your neural pathways are set because you literally feel you're in a rut.

When brain ruts develop, your thoughts get 'railroaded'. I once accidentally drove my car onto tramlines in Melbourne, Victoria, and its wheels got stuck in the rail ruts. The car then started following the tracks, which was disconcerting at first but then I started to have fun with it. Taking my hands off the steering wheel, the car drove through the city as if on autopilot. It also took some effort to wrench the car off the tracks when a tram approached.

The processes of Neuro-Linguistic Programming (NLP) are based on a similar principle. NLP aims to change the brain ruts that have formed through years and years of the same thought processes flowing through your head. For instance, tell yourself a thousand times a day you're no good, you're weak, you're insignificant, and guess how you'll feel at the end of the day? Tell yourself a thousand times a day you're okay, you're doing just fine, you're bigger than you think you are, and guess how you'll feel at the end of the day?

The brain as we know is malleable, as stroke rehabilitation has shown. Its neural pathways can be rerouted and diverted around parts that aren't working any more. Sometimes, though, our strokes are not necessarily physical ones, they're psychological.

These psychological strokes are mind gaps that have been starved of mental nutrients and are now dysfunctional. When a part of our consciousness is neglected for periods of time, that part can wither and suffocate, just as if an artery has clogged and deprived oxygen to a section of the brain. When thoughts just travel in one direction, following one path for years on end, these thoughts can only feed the part of your mind to which they flow. Thoughts, ideas, and images are mind food—they provide nutrients to your mind—and so any part of the mind that gets neglected because your thoughts are channelled only to selected areas can suffer because of that neglect.

A healthy mind is a mind fed with more than just one type of thought. Just as you should eat five fresh fruits and vegetables each day to get the required nutrition your body needs, so too your mind needs a variety of thoughts, ideas, and images to stay healthy and function optimally.

Of course, it's preferable that these thoughts, ideas, and images produce a fit and healthy vision of who you are—your ideal you. Eaten daily produces the best results. Eaten fresh is even better. Stale ideas only produce stale results. Constant reinvention, constant rethinking, produces vibrancy, energy, and a sense of aliveness.

A bigger and better you

YELLOW DIAMOND PRACTICE—EMPOWER YOUR BELIEFS

Because your thoughts determine your feelings and behaviours, any self-limiting belief will cause you to feel self-limiting emotions and to behave in self-limiting or self-sabotaging ways. Your mottos and beliefs, however, are part of an even bigger story you tell yourself.

But because it's a story, it can be rewritten, which requires a change in dialogue from self-limiting to self-empowering. Self-empowering beliefs will cause you to feel empowering emotions and to take empowered action.

There are many belief changing tools, but one of the best tools to change self-limiting beliefs is The Wheel of Change.[39] This belief changing tool acts quickly and bypasses the three main barriers to change: your thoughts, emotions, and instincts.

Here is the 7-step process to change any self-limiting belief into a self-empowering belief:

1. *Why* is this belief 100% true?
2. *When* has this belief not been true?
3. *What* effect does this belief have?
4. *Who* will you be in 5-7 years with this belief still in place?
5. *Where* will this belief take you in 5-7 years if it isn't changed?
6. *How* would your life change without that limiting belief?
7. *Now* is the time to change!

---

[39] The Wheel of Change belief changing tool is a modification of multiple psychological and life-coaching tools available. I have created this tool to simplify the process of changing your self-limiting beliefs to those that are more empowering.

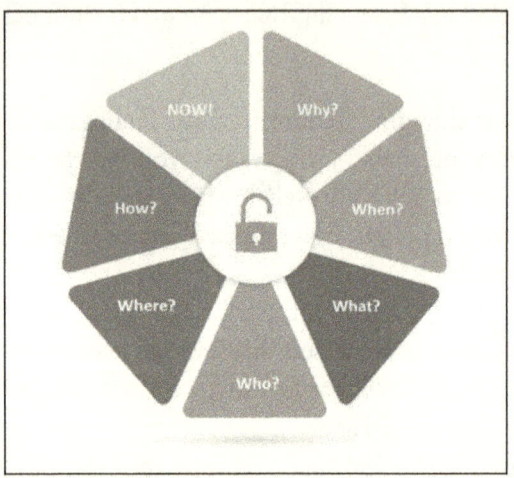

FIGURE 23:   The Wheel of Change

Let's use an example of how you can use this tool to change a self-limiting belief. For instance, you might believe that you're not good enough to apply for that job or promotion you really want. The first question to ask is:

Why is this belief 100% true?

This is actually a trick question. It's designed to make you realise that this could not possibly be 100% true. If you really do believe it's true, you have to provide evidence that it is, which you can't do because there is at least one time in your life when this belief is not supported by any factual evidence.

Which leads to the second question:

When has this belief not been true?

Once you have admitted that this belief is not 100% true all the time, you are forced to concede that there are times when the opposite was true, that you are good enough for that job or promotion.

However, this self-limiting belief has consequences, which the third question forces you to consider:

What effect does this belief have?

The effect is probably negative. It probably means that you don't apply for the job or promotion, and so you remain where you are and don't progress in your career. So, what will happen if you still cling to this belief? This is the fourth question:

Who will you be in 5-7 years with this belief still in place?

Project yourself into the future and imagine who you've become and what you'll be doing whilst still holding onto this belief. Will this belief allow you to become the person you were born to be and fulfil your true potential?

The fifth question goes one step further:

Where will this belief take you in 5-7 years if it isn't changed?

Will this belief allow you to do what you've always wanted to do? Has this belief led you to your niche, or are you stuck in a rut and despairing that nothing is going to change?

The sixth question then asks you to consider what might happen if things were different:

How would your life change without that limiting belief?

What does your future look like now that you've let that belief go? Have you been promoted? Have you been headhunted by another firm, a firm that you always thought was beyond you? Think not just of your career, but also the benefits to your partner and family, your health, finances, and emotional wellbeing.

The final step in the process is to act immediately:

Now is the time to change!

Like goal setting, changing old beliefs works best when you think on paper. If your old belief was that you aren't good enough for that job or promotion, your new belief will be: *I am good enough for that job/promotion. I can do this!*

The power of 'I Am. I Will. I Can.' is at work here. But it amplifies when you write it down. It's also best if you write it on a business card or similar sized piece of paper that you can put in your purse or wallet and review it at every mealtime over the next 21 days (more if you need to).

The act of thinking the new belief activates the neurones and connections in your right brain. The act of writing the new belief activates the neurones and connections in your left brain. The act of reviewing the new belief—reading it, thinking it, saying it, feeling it—energises the right and left brain, creating new connections that bypass the barriers of your triune brain. You have now established a new empowering belief.

But it takes at least 21 days for these new connections to become myelinated and fixed. Which is why you need to ensure you review your new belief constantly. Then, before you know it, you will find that you are good enough for that job or promotion and living your being.

PART 4

LIFE LEADERSHIP
PRACTICES

TIER #2: SUCCESS

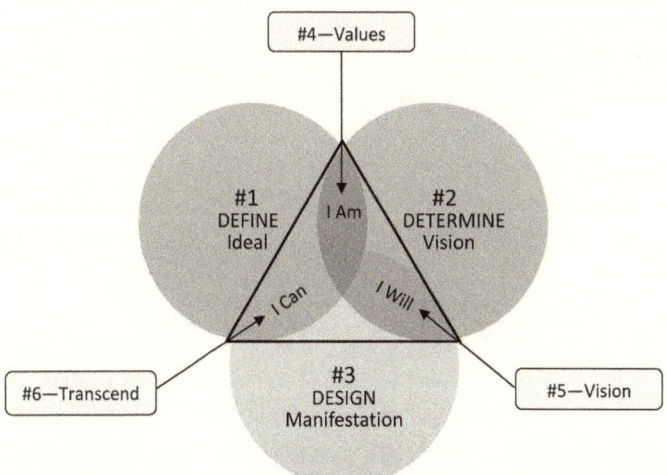

11 BLUE DIAMOND: REFINE YOUR VALUES

LIFE LEADERSHIP PRACTICE #4

THE NEXT LEVEL of your Life Leadership journey is blue diamond. The aim of this level is to attain success-level knowledge of Life Skill #1–Who, and progress to red diamond level within 3-4 months. The practice of refining your values is the second in the process of 'Realigning' and moving into Quadrant #1 in the Empowered Living Index.

The core of this Life Leadership Practice is to understand how your values strongly influence your success and prosperity. In The Diamond Triangle, your values form the second of three building blocks in your 'I Am' axis, and is now looking like this:

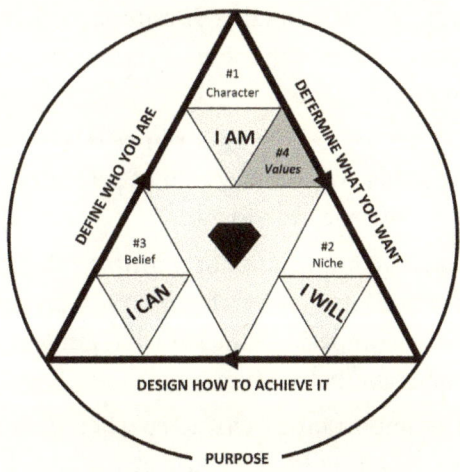

FIGURE 24: Blue Diamond—Values

IT'S UP TO YOU!

Your values tell the world what you stand for and provide you with a personal code of conduct. Just as your mottos reveal your underlying beliefs, your values are an indication of the worth you place upon certain attitudes and behaviours. What you value in yourself and others, what worth you assign to certain principles, is a measure of who you are, or at least who you aspire to be. Values are the ideals to which you hold yourself accountable and thereby determine the ethical standards by which you live.

Psychologist Shalom Schwartz is the creator of the Theory of Basic Human Values and The Schwartz Value Survey. He has defined values as a 'collection of guiding principles' that determine what we deem as correct and desirable. He outlines values in the following terms:[40]

1. Values are beliefs that are linked to affect. When values are activated, they are infused with emotion.
2. Values refer to desirable goals that motivate action.
3. Values transcend specific actions and situations (that is, they have a general impact).
4. Values serve as standards or criteria, which guide the selection or evaluation of actions, policies, people, and events.
5. Values are ordered by importance relative to one another to form a system of priorities that characterise the individual.
6. The relative importance of multiple values guides our action, whereby the trade-off between relevant, competing values is what guides our attitudes and behaviours.

Values are as important as character when defining who you are and your success. Life Leaders have clarity on what they value

[40] Shalom Schwartz, *A Theory of Cultural Value Orientations: Explication and Applications*, Comparative Sociology, Brill, 2006

and how their values influence their thoughts, emotions and behaviours. When you consistently honour your values through living them, you experience fulfilment and a heightened quality of life. You experience less stress and greater peace of mind. You experience greater harmony between who you are being and what you are doing.

We will now discuss values in relation to:

1. Community values
2. Personal values
3. Core values

COMMUNITY VALUES

Community values are those values you believe best suit the local and national community in which you live. They are the rules, the philosophies, the rights to which you agree to live by in accordance with the laws of the land. They determine how you see yourself as a community, as a nation, as a culture.

Some examples of community values include:

COMMUNITY VALUES	
Democracy	Diversity
Freedom of speech	Right to life
Religious freedom and tolerance	Abortion
Equality (sex, race, age, marriage)	Right to bear arms
Justice and liberty	Rule of law

TABLE 22: Community Values

We gravitate to those cultures and countries that support the same values we have. In this way, who we are is encouraged and supported by the community in which we live. If our values change over time, we are either brought back into line by the community around us (for instance, through penalties, fines, imprisonment, exclusion), or we pack our bags and move to another community and culture that supports our new values.

Examples of community groups that uphold and support certain values include church groups, political parties, charities, not for profit organisations, sports clubs, the armed forces, schools, and universities. Extreme examples of community groups include religious sects, bikie clubs, mafia, drug gangs, and terrorist organisations.

Consider the different communities that you belong to and associate with. Do you share common values? Are these values truly representative of who you are? Are these values viable?

It's okay if your values adapt over time. Things change. Events happen. Your life-situation moves on. Just be sure your community values reflect the true core of who you are.

PERSONAL VALUES

Personal values are those values you believe best suit yourself. They are the ideals, the beliefs, the principles to which you hold as a standard to live up to. They determine how you see yourself as a person, as an individual, as a human being. They are the values you hope will shape you into the person you want to be and to be remembered by.

Some examples of personal values are shown in *Table 23: Personal Values*. We are attracted to partners and friends who share the same personal values as we do. Birds of a feather flock together. Like the natural human need to belong to a community, there's a degree of safety and security in knowing that your ideals and principles are agreed with, reinforced, and appreciated by those who are closest to you. People like seeing themselves in others, and relationships flourish when beliefs and attitudes are mirrored.

PERSONAL VALUES	
Selflessness and courage	Purpose and meaning
Charity and gratitude	Leadership and teamwork
Fairness and forgiveness	Love and kindness
Religion and spirituality	Appreciation of beauty
Honesty and humility	Humour and hope
Wisdom and patience	Passion and creativity

TABLE 23:   Personal Values

On the flipside, relationships struggle when personal values conflict, or when one partner's values changes. Opposites may attract for a while, but a wife with a strong work ethic won't stay married to a husband with a lazy attitude. Two atheists may be happy with their relationship until such a time one partner grows spiritually and begins seeking an outlet for their new beliefs. Friendships may drift apart when honesty and loyalty are challenged and found to be insufficient.

Shared personal values are probably more important and impactful than shared community values, simply because the degree of personal contact and the amount of time in contact with those closest to you are so much greater than with your community. Take a moment then to consider the people closest to you. Do you share common values? Are these values truly representative of who you are? Are your values compatible with mutual growth?

CORE VALUES

Core Values unite your community and personal values. If community values and personal values are two ends of a bow tie, then Core Values are the knot in the middle. Core Values are the reason behind the ideals, the why behind the beliefs. Core Values are the seed from which all other values grow and flower.

Although there are thousands of community and personal values, there are only three Core Values. These are the common, motivating forces of all people, the shared human needs we all experience. They are:

1. Goodness
2. Truth
3. Beauty

Since the time of Plato, Goodness, Truth and Beauty have been the three noble principles of humanity. There are no higher values than these. There are no more powerful values. Society over the ages has divided itself along these three lines as religion (Goodness), science (Truth), and art (Beauty). Each is simply an attempt at describing reality. None is better than the other. Like all forms of communication, religion, science and art are simply an expression, a language, that seeks to show how goodness triumphs over evil, truth prevails over ignorance, and beauty shines through suffering.[41]

As Einstein once said:

> *The ideals which have always shone before me and filled me with the joy of living are goodness, beauty, and truth.*[42]

---

[41] Science, Art and Religion are the three 'noble' languages that humanity uses to describe the three levels in which the universe works and functions—these are cause and effect, synchronicity, and miracles respectively.

[42] Albert Einstein, *Einstein on Politics: His Private Thoughts and Public Stand on Nationalism, Zionism, War, Peace, and the Bomb*, Princeton University Press, 2013

BLUE DIAMOND: REFINE YOUR VALUES

Just as all our fears are adaptations of our three primal fears of abandonment, falling, and loud noises, no matter what principles and ideals you believe in and stand for, every one of them stems from the three Core Values of Goodness, Truth and Beauty. All your principles and ideals are therefore expressions or manifestations of its underlying Core Value.

Table 24: Core Values—Goodness, Truth & Beauty, illustrates the connection between Core Values and all other values.

PERSONAL VALUE	CORE VALUE	COMMUNITY VALUE
Selflessness and courage	**GOODNESS**	Tolerance
Charity and gratitude		Democracy
Fairness and forgiveness		Fraternity
Religion/Spirituality		Religious freedom
Honesty and humility	**TRUTH**	Justice
Wisdom and patience		Rule of law
Purpose and meaning		Freedom of speech
Leadership and teamwork		Right to life/ Human rights
Love and kindness	**BEAUTY**	Liberty
Appreciation of beauty and Love of learning		Equality
Humour and hope		Inclusivity
Passion and creativity		Diversity

TABLE 24: Core Values—Goodness, Truth & Beauty

Within each personal and community value is a seed of Goodness, Truth or Beauty. Commitment to these Core Values can be life defining. When you commit to Goodness, Truth and Beauty, you in fact define yourself along those lines, as a seeker, a pilgrim, a lover. When you identify with them, they become your heart, mind, and soul.

When considering your Core Values, the best way to know if they are right for you is to test their strength and validity by asking this question:

> *Are my Core Values a reliable inner compass with which I can navigate my journey through this lifetime to who I want to be and what I want to achieve?*

BLUE DIAMOND: REFINE YOUR VALUES

BLUE DIAMOND PRACTICE—YOUR VALUE STATEMENT

The exercise for blue diamond level is to develop and write your Value Statement. There are three steps to achieve this:

1. The Value Circle—identifying your value strengths and weaknesses.
2. The Value Pack—identifying your top 7 values.
3. Value Clarification—writing a concise and clear Value Statement.

The Value Circle

The Value Circle is designed to help you identify your value strengths and weaknesses. It is divided into 7 segments:

- Family & Relationships
- Career & Work
- Money & Finances
- Health & Wellbeing
- Learning & Education
- Fun & Adventure
- Spirituality & Ethics

Your task is to rate each segment on a scale of 0-10 (where 0 is the lowest and 10 is the highest). For instance, you might rate Family & Relationships as 9 or 10, but Money & Finances as 3. Do this for all segments and consider how each is being honoured in your life.

Does this reveal any insights that you were not previously aware?

IT'S UP TO YOU!

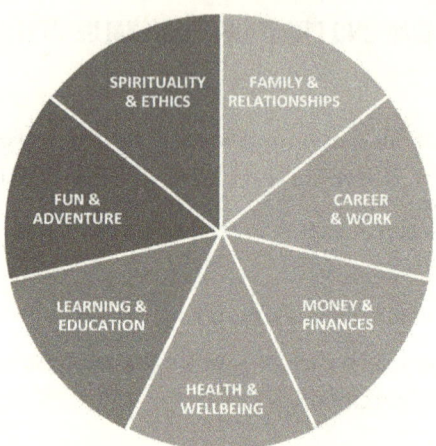

FIGURE 25: The Value Circle

The Value Pack

The Value Pack is a comprehensive list of values that you can use to identify your top 7 values. Directions for using the Value Pack are:

-> Cross out or eliminate the values that you consider low or zero importance.

-> Circle or highlight the values that you consider very high importance.

-> If you have not circled or highlighted 7 very high important values, go through the list and add more values to total 7. These will not necessarily be very high important values, but they will be high important values.

-> Ensure that you have at least 1 value circled or highlighted in each column.

-> Review your very high and high important values and choose 1 from each column.

-> Rank these 7 important values from 1-7 (1 highest, 7 lowest).

BLUE DIAMOND: REFINE YOUR VALUES

FAMILY & RELATIONSHIPS	CAREER & WORK	MONEY & FINANCES	HEALTH & WELLBEING	LEARNING & EDUCATION	FUN & ADVENTURE	SPIRITUALITY & ETHICS
Belonging	Advancement	Autonomy	Meaning	Challenge	Adventure	Beauty
Patience	Competence	Financial Gain	Personal Expression	Knowledge	Change	Arts
Communication	Achievement	Location	Self-respect	Curiosity	Creativity	Democracy
Community	Fame	Power	Stability	Mastery	Leisure	Diversity
Cooperation	Prestige	Sophistication	Peace	Truth	Excitement	Religion
Love	Productivity	Security	Structure	Wisdom	Openness	Fairness
Loyalty	Teamwork	Status	Joy	Education	Variety	Honesty
Privacy	Reputation	Stability	Harmony	Collaboration	Nature	Quality
Recognition	Merit	Wealth	Humour	Innovation	Freedom	Spirituality
Friendship	Influence	Legacy	Wellbeing	Intellect	Fun	Goodness
Forgiveness	Balance	Philanthropy	Gratitude	Equality	Pleasure	Mercy

TABLE 25: The Value Pack

IT'S UP TO YOU!

Value Clarification

Now that you have listed your top 7 values, you can now write your Value Statement. Be as concise as you can in three sentences. Try also to evoke emotion in your statement because that will employ both right side and left side of your brain in the process.

Here is a simple template to write your Value Statement:

1. My passion is [fill blank] and I believe my life purpose as a [fill blank] is to...
2. I value [state your top 3 values] and I dedicate myself to these values through [state action/behaviours]...
3. I believe [state belief type value or meaning], which is best expressed through [state action/behaviour/purpose]...

Feel free to use my Value Statement as an example:

> *My passion is writing, and I believe my life purpose as a messenger is to help others achieve their life purpose through coaching and mentorship. I value Goodness, Truth and Beauty and dedicate myself to these values through Giving, Forgiving, and Thanksgiving. I believe my natural state of being is joyous, acceptable, secure, peaceful, and free—and these are expressed best through living my being.*

The more aligned you are with your values, the more happiness and wellbeing you experience. So ask yourself these questions at least weekly, if not daily:

1. Does my behaviour honour and demonstrate my values?
2. Am I true to my values?
3. Are there ways I can better align my thoughts, emotions, and behaviours with my values?

12 RED DIAMOND: RETAIN YOUR VISION

LIFE LEADERSHIP PRACTICE #5

THE NEXT LEVEL of your Life Leadership journey is red diamond. The aim of this level is to attain success-level knowledge of Life Skill #3–What, and progress to black diamond level within 3-4 months. The practice of retaining your vision is the second in the process of 'Reconnecting' and moving into Quadrant #1 in the Empowered Living Index.

The core of this Life Leadership Practice is to determine the goals you need to keep true to the vison of who you are and what you want to achieve. In The Diamond Triangle, retaining your vision is the second building block in your 'I Will' axis, and is now looking like this:

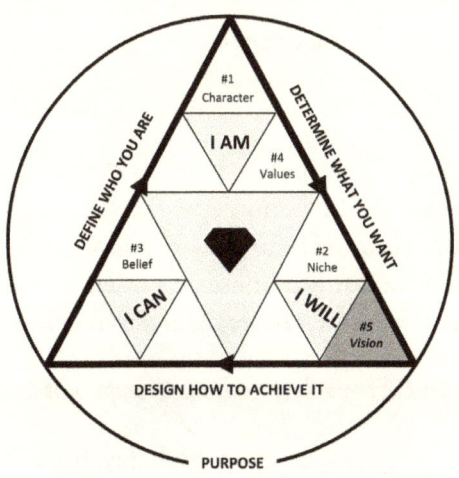

FIGURE 26: Red Diamond—Vision

IT'S UP TO YOU!

In our discussion on goal setting in Chapter 6, we discussed the benefits of thinking on paper and writing down your goals to Generate motivation, Overcome obstacles, Account for action, Leverage time, money, resources, and effort, and Specify results (GOALS). Proper goal setting prevents procrastination and minimises stress. Goal setting also greatly increases your chances of success and achieving the outcomes you want.

We will now discuss in more detail the specifics of goal setting, how to set goals that are best for you, and how to realign those goals with your values and your vision of who you are.

HOW TO SET GOALS

There are many great books on how to set goals, so without wanting to repeat what's already available for you, I'm just going to highlight the important elements of goal setting:

- Think Big, Act Small
- Don't Compare, Don't Compete
- Work Backwards to Go Forwards
- Take Action, Take the Shot

<u>Think Big, Act Small</u>

Goal setting should incorporate your short-term plans with your long-term objectives. They should be the stepping stones toward your big picture vision of who you are and what you want to do. Like a bricklayer building a house one brick at a time, achieving many small goals builds your dream and makes it a reality:

Your dreams are reached with small steps, not large leaps.

When you were young, you probably drew 'join the dot' pictures. You would start at dot number 1, draw a line to dot 2,

RED DIAMOND: RETAIN YOUR VISION

then a line to dot 3, then dot 4 and dot 5, and all the way to dot 50 or more. At the last dot you would have drawn a picture of an animal, or person, or a scene. All from single lines drawn from dot to dot.

Goal setting is like that. When you set small goals and join them up one after another, you complete the big picture vision you have for yourself.

You should also make your goals simple enough to accomplish within a reasonable timeframe, like to-do lists. One of the greatest motivating factors is seeing reward for your actions, and achieving small goals ups your confidence and strengthens your self-belief.

However, act small but don't think small. Life coaches tell us we overestimate what we can do in a day, but underestimate what we can achieve in a lifetime. Although your goals should be small and simple, your mission and your vision should be on a grand scale.

Set low and achievable goals but aim your vision high and reach for the stars.

Don't Compare, Don't Compete

Everyone is on their own journey, so don't compare yourself to others. You'll always find people who are not as good as you at some things, don't have as much money, or aren't as smart. But you'll always find people who are better at you than some things, have more money, or are smarter than you.

Setting and completing goals puts you on a path of constant improvement and learning, as long as you don't compare your life or what you're doing with others. There's no comparison between the sun and the moon—they shine when it's their time.

The best competition is therefore the competition you have with yourself. Compare yourself now to where you've come from, and then set your sights on what you can be in the future.

IT'S UP TO YOU!

<u>Work Backwards to Go Forwards</u>

Setting goals is easier when you work backwards from the end. When you know the end result you want to achieve, you can reverse engineer your way to your current situation.

For instance, if you want to take a cruise next summer, you might need to save $5000 for the holiday. That's the bigger mission you've set yourself, and you can break it down into doable goals. Working backwards from the date of your holiday in 12 months, you can set financial goals you need to reach by certain timeframes. In 9 months you will need to have saved $3750. In 6 months you will need to have saved half the amount, $2500. In 3 months, $1250. You can break this down further into weekly amounts, which is about $100.

Saving $100 per week will put you on track to saving $5000 in 1 year, as long as you stay disciplined and hold yourself accountable to putting $100 away every single week.

That's how you work backwards to go forwards.

<u>Take Action, Take the Shot</u>

Goals that stay in your head are just dreams. Goals written down are actionable items. But if you don't take the necessary action to achieve your goals, they will remain just thoughts on paper. This is the silent rule in play again, Rule #4: Deliver It.

So don't let yourself get in the way of your dreams. Take note of your thoughts, emotions, and instincts when setting your goals. Many goals don't get achieved because of self-doubt, fear, and hesitancy. Many books don't get written. Many trips don't get taken. Many promotions don't get accepted. Many relationships don't get started.

As ice hockey star, Wayne Gretzky, said:

You miss 100% of the shots you don't take.

RED DIAMOND: RETAIN YOUR VISION

Take action. Take the shot. You never know what might happen. You might just score that goal.

THE BEST GOALS ARE OWN GOALS

In the game of soccer, scoring an own goal is a severe blunder. It's hard enough to score a goal for your own team, but to hand the opposition a gift makes winning so much more difficult.

Yet I say the best goals are own goals. The goals that you set for your own personal and professional life, of course: individual goals, relationship goals, and career goals. When setting goals, balance is always the best option. Too much focus on material or financial gain, for instance, can result in disillusionment. As we know, only 10% of your happiness is influenced by your circumstances, but 40% by your voluntary choices.

So balance is the key, and to achieve a balanced life you need balanced goals. This is where your values step in, because they give you balance. It's also why you were asked to do the practice exercise for blue diamond and clarify your values. Clarification of your values gives you a framework with which you can prepare a balanced set of goals. It also gives you the 'why' you want to achieve these particular goals.

Use The Value Circle (*Figure 25: The Value Circle*) in the blue diamond practice now to establish a balance in the 7 main areas or segments of your life.

<u>Family & Relationships</u>

The need to belong is an ingrained human need. It's part of your DNA. You feel better and your wellbeing improves when you feel connected to others in a meaningful way. There is a vast bank of research that tells us when people feel connected, loved, and accepted, their health outcomes are far superior to those who feel disconnected, unloved, and unworthy.

This includes partners, family, friends, neighbours, work colleagues, teammates, and any other social environment you engage with. All these relationships are an important factor in your health and wellbeing. Although it takes two to tango, you can control, to some degree, the strength of every relationship you have through the strength of your desire and willingness to connect with people.

Reference the score you gave yourself on Family & Relationships (0-10) in The Value Circle exercise in the previous chapter. If you scored low, your goals for this segment will best reflect the areas of improvement you want to make, such as better communication and listening. If you scored high, your goals will best reflect the areas in which you wish to maintain and flourish.

Goals you might set for Family & Relationships include:

- Creating more time to spend with loved ones.
- Responding with kindness instead of reacting with irritation and anger.
- Joining a sports team.
- Volunteering for a charity.
- Being more forgiving of other's actions and mistakes.

Because forgiveness heals even the oldest wounds.

Career & Work

For many, work is just a means to an end. It pays the bills and puts food on the table. Or it doesn't, so you need two jobs and must work 60 or more hours a week to make ends meet.

There is an average of 110-120 waking hours per week, so for something that uses 30-50% of your waking hours, it really should be spent on something that you love to do. Otherwise you are just surviving, not thriving. Is this possible? Is it realistic to do something that you are passionate about and still pay the bills and put food on the table?

It's up to you. It's up to the choices you make and the desire you have to make it real. It's up to the values you have and the beliefs you hold true about life and your power to manifest the reality you want. If you don't believe it's possible, it might be good to revisit The Wheel of Change belief changing tool in the practice for yellow diamond. Thinking on paper will help to put things in perspective.

Then reference the score you gave yourself on Career & Work (0-10) in The Value Circle exercise. If you scored low, your goals for this segment will best reflect the areas of improvement you want to make, such as changing your beliefs about what you can achieve. If you scored high, your goals will best reflect the areas in which you wish to maintain and flourish.

Goals you might set for Career & Work include:

- Work-life balance.
- Upskilling and further training.
- Identifying your purpose and passion in life.
- Advancement and promotional opportunities.
- Reassessing your remuneration and pay.

Because you should get paid for what you're worth.

Money & Finances

Although money and finances might not be your cup of tea, remember that everything has a cost—you either pay with time or with money. As time is your most valuable resource, I recommend you focus on paying with money. Don't spend time to save money.

Everyone will have different financial needs depending on their individual circumstances and where they live. Your current stage of life, state of health, family, work, transport, and other costs of living determine the minimum amount you must earn to prevent slipping into debt. However, the money you currently have in your bank account isn't a reflection of today's choices; it's a reflection of

IT'S UP TO YOU!

the choices you've made up until this point in time. What you see in your bank statement is a lag, a time lapse, of what has happened in the past. The choices you make today will be reflected in the future.

Sarah K. was a client who came to me with a quandary. Although in her late twenties, she was still living at home and dependent on her parents for support. But she wanted to break free from her controlling father and move to another city, where she felt she could finally be herself. The challenge she faced was money. She had no savings and any money that came her way was drip fed to her from her father.

After discussing the financials of moving cities, we developed a plan of savings that would get her to a target of $6000 that she felt was doable over the next 6 months. She got a job as a waitress and began saving $250 per week. What had seemed like a daunting figure to begin with was made achievable by breaking it down into bite-sized chunks and giving her belief that it was possible.

For others, moving cities is not on the cards, but buying a house and planning for retirement are. These are probably going to be your two biggest investments in your lifetime, but the process is the same as Sarah's. Financial advisors will tell you to work out how much you predict you will need in retirement—mortgage, food, transport, utilities, medical—then factor in contingency amounts for unseen costs and any other costs for leisure and entertainment. That total sum is the figure you set yourself to have in savings and investments by the time you retire. Then you make a plan and set goals on how to reach that figure.

Reference the score you gave yourself on Money & Finances (0-10) in The Value Circle exercise. If you scored low, your goals for this segment will best reflect the areas of improvement you want to make, such as a financial plan for retirement. If you scored high, your goals will best reflect the areas in which you wish to maintain and flourish.

Goals you might set for Money & Finance include:

- Mortgage deposit and repayments.
- Retirement planning and wealth creation.
- Passive income and investments.
- Legacy and will.
- Leisure and travel.

Because you've already won the biggest lottery there is—life. It's now up to you how you spend it.

Health & Wellbeing

Just as your past choices affect the wealth in your bank account, so too your past choices affect the health of your wellbeing account. Your current physical, mental, and spiritual health reflects the choices you've made up until this point in time. Apart from serious illness, for which you should always seek medical advice, your general health and wellbeing is a time lapse of what you've done, or haven't done, in the past.

For instance, doctors estimate that for every 1 kilogram (2.2 pounds) of excess fat in your body, your heart has to pump the equivalent of 3.55 kilometres (2.2 miles) through extra blood vessels every day. If you are 10 kilograms overweight, that's 35 kilometres (22 miles) of extra pumping your heart has to do each day. That's about 13,000 extra kilometres (8,000 miles) each year, or about the same distance as a return flight from London to Chicago.

Wellbeing is also mental, emotional, and spiritual. Reference the score you gave yourself on Health & Wellbeing (0-10) in The Value Circle exercise. If you scored low, your goals for this segment will best reflect the areas of improvement you want to make, such as a fitness plan for losing weight or planning a holiday for rest and relaxation. If you scored high, your goals will best reflect the areas in which you wish to maintain and flourish.

Goals you might set for Health & Wellbeing include:

- Healthier eating and nutrition.
- Lowering caffeine and alcohol consumption.
- Increased physical exercise and fitness.
- Attending yoga and meditation classes.
- Getting back to nature.
- Reducing time watching TV and on electronic devices.
- Being more grateful for the little things that come your way.

Because the happiest people in life are the most grateful people in life.

Learning & Education

Because life is a full-time education, there isn't a time when the opportunity to learn something new isn't available.

When you learn, you grow. But anything that limits your growth has a negative effect on your sense of being. Boredom is a tell-tale sign, a symptom, that you've stopped learning. This isn't the boredom you hear in the backseat of the car, 'There's nothing to do!' It's the boredom of believing you know everything there is to know, the inevitable consequence of convincing yourself that there's nothing new, nothing fresh, nor will there ever be. It's the staleness you feel when you think there's nothing left to learn in life.

Some people feel this in their job or their relationship, and there's even a term for it: the '7-Year Itch'. Some people even feel this about themselves. They are bored with their work, their partner, and with their life. But when you develop a passion for learning, the zest of life returns. There's joy in learning new things. There's fun in discovering something new. Learning fertilises personal growth.

RED DIAMOND: RETAIN YOUR VISION

Reference the score you gave yourself on Learning & Education (0-10) in The Value Circle exercise. If you scored low, your goals for this segment will best reflect the areas of improvement you want to make, such as opening your mind to the possibilities of learning something new every day. If you scored high, your goals will best reflect the areas in which you wish to maintain and flourish.

Goals you might set for Learning & Education include:

- Finding new challenges and opportunities for personal development.
- Striving for mastery in your area of speciality.
- Learning a new language or musical instrument.
- Enrolling in a subject that you've always wanted to learn.
- Offering to teach or mentor students or junior colleagues.

Because teaching is the best way to learn.

Fun & Adventure

One of my daughter's preschool teachers once remarked that, in all her 30 years of experience with young families, the thing that struck her most was that parents had forgotten how to play. Adults, it seems, have lost the ability to have fun.

The needs of everyday life can blind us to the inherent joy of life and limit our sense of adventure. Children don't have this problem. Just look at every primary school playground at lunchtime. As adults, though, we can become very serious creatures. Yet some would claim that life is far too important to take seriously.

There is a large body of research showing how chronic anger, hostility, and worry increases the risk of heart disease and poor health. On the contrary, having fun and experiencing happiness has been shown to be protective of your heart. It also strengthens your immune system, reduces stress, minimises bodily aches and pains, combats disease and disability. It even has a positive effect on your lifespan and improves relationships. Laughter really is the best medicine.

Reference the score you gave yourself on Fun & Adventure (0-10) in The Value Circle exercise. If you scored low, your goals for this segment will best reflect the areas of improvement you want to make, such doing something fun at least once a day. If you scored high, your goals will best reflect the areas in which you wish to maintain and flourish.

Goals you might set for Fun & Adventure include:

- Booking that holiday you've been wanting to take for a long time.
- Saying 'Yes!' more often to invitations to go out.
- Spending more time outdoors.
- Finding the humour in life's drama.
- Smiling and laughing more.

Because a smile a day keeps the doctor at bay.

Spirituality & Ethics

Spirituality & Ethics is a broad subject that covers a wide range of ideas and beliefs, but for our purposes we will simply consider it as the human spirit. You can call it the soul, if you like, or even your own human nature. But how you define your human spirit is up to you; there is no right or wrong in this.

Personally, I like any definition of the human spirit that includes Goodness, Truth and Beauty. When you connect with acts of Goodness, ideas of Truth, and things of Beauty, you are in fact connecting with your innate human spirit. If passion is what your purpose feels like, then Goodness, Truth and Beauty is what *you* feel like at the core of who you are—your essential beingness.

You know this to be true in your own experience. When you do good for someone else and help them in some way, you feel good about it. The act of giving releases the goodness in your heart and you feel a lightness of being, a kind of natural high.

When you hear a truth, it 'rings true' to you. You don't need factual evidence for this truth, you just *know it* to be true. It lifts you to another level of awareness and understanding. In this sense, the truth sets you free.

When you see a thing of beauty, you are captured by its spell. It takes your breath away. You sense a timelessness, as if for a moment time stops, and you carry that timeless moment—that essence—as a memory for the rest of your life.

Reference the score you gave yourself on Spirituality & Ethics (0-10) in The Value Circle exercise. If you scored low, your goals for this segment will best reflect the areas of improvement you want to make, such as seeking more experiences of Goodness, Truth and Beauty. If you scored high, your goals will best reflect the areas in which you wish to maintain and flourish.

Goals you might set for Spirituality & Ethics could include:

- Dedicating yourself to honesty and integrity.
- Volunteering for a charity or good cause.
- Focussing on the underlying beauty of life and not its external ugliness.
- Pausing for a few minutes a day to be present in the moment.

Because this moment of now is all you have.

IT'S UP TO YOU!

RED DIAMOND PRACTICE—THE RETAINED MODEL

The exercise for red diamond level is to retain the vision of who you are and what you want to achieve. This practice involves the application of The RETAINED Model™, a personal development tool that aligns your vision and goals with your values. Because when your vision, goals, and values are aligned, you are in harmonious balance with who you are being and what you are doing.

The RETAINED Model™ is a simple but powerful realignment exercise where your task is to consider the ideal vision of who you *want to be* and what *you want to do*. To do this, make a list in *Table 26: Value Criteria*, in order of importance from top to bottom, these eight Value Criteria:

- R: Remuneration
- E: Education
- T: Trust
- A: Appreciation
- I: Influence
- N: New Opportunities
- E: Empowerment
- D: Direction

The table is divided into three Vital, three Important, and two Bonus criteria. You might list remuneration (e.g. income), new promotional opportunities and education as 'Vital' criteria for your ideal vision of who you want to be and what you want to do. Then you might have trust, appreciation and personal empowerment as 'Important' criteria. Lastly, you might have direction and being a person of influence as 'Bonus' criteria.

You have now created a list of value prioritisation. Now consider whether these criteria are being met in your current situation. This can include your current relationships and even your role at work. Put a tick or a cross in the 'Yes' or 'No' columns next to each criterion. Now assign a numerical value of 4 to the Vital criteria, 2 to the Important criteria, and 1 to the Bonus criteria.

	VALUE CRITERIA	YES	NO
VITAL	1.		
VITAL	2.		
VITAL	3.		
IMPORTANT	4.		
IMPORTANT	5.		
IMPORTANT	6.		
BONUS	7.		
BONUS	8.		

TABLE 26: Value Criteria

Add up how many ticks you have in the 'Yes' column that correlate to your Vital criteria and give yourself a score out of 12. For instance, if you have two ticks in this field, then you score 8/12. No ticks equal 0/12.

Do the same with the number of ticks correlating to your Important criteria and score it out of 6. For instance, if you have one tick in this field, then you score 2/6.

Do the same with the number of ticks correlating to your Bonus values and score it out of 2. For instance, if you have two ticks in this field, then you score 2/2.

Finally, tally up your scores and give yourself a total score out of 20. For instance, one vital tick, three important ticks, and two bonus ticks gives you a total score of 4 + 6 + 2 = 12/20.

The score you achieve the first time you do this exercise represents your standardised score, the score that you compare to when you do this exercise again in the future. There is no right or wrong with this exercise. It's simply a gauge as to where you see yourself in this moment.

IT'S UP TO YOU!

If you scored 15/20 or more, that's fantastic. It probably means you're on the right track. All you need to work on is satisfying your Bonus criteria.

If you scored 11-14/20, you're probably comfortable with where you're at. But you would do well to sit down and work on how to satisfy your Vital and Important criteria, or even re-evaluate the level of importance of your criteria.

If you scored 10/20 and under, however, this could indicate a malalignment with who you are and what you do. It is an indication that your values and expectations are not being met. You owe it to yourself to sit down and discuss your current situation with a partner or close friend, and whether there is scope for your Vital and Important criteria to be met in your current situation.

The payoff for retaining your vision will be worth it.

13 BLACK DIAMOND: TRANSCEND YOUR AWARENESS

LIFE LEADERSHIP PRACTICE #6

CONGRATULATIONS! YOU HAVE now reached the level of Life Leadership mastery, black diamond. The aim of this level is to attain success-level knowledge of Life Skill #2–Why, and progress to green diamond level within 3-4 months. The practice of transcending your awareness is the second in the process of 'Rejuvenating' and moving into Quadrant #1 in the Empowered Living Index.

The core of this Life Leadership Practice is to create and maintain a harmonious balance between all levels of consciousness—sub-conscious, conscious, and supra-conscious. In The Diamond Triangle, transcending your awareness is the second building block in your 'I Can' axis, and is now looking like this:

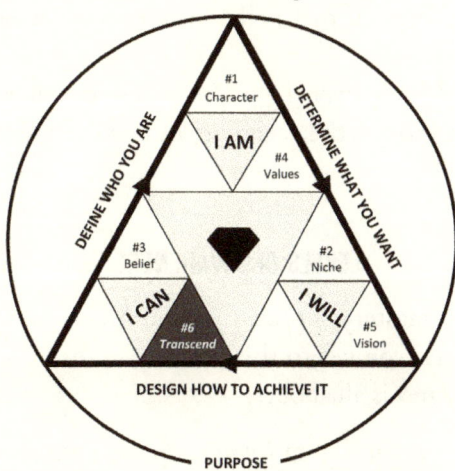

FIGURE 27:   Black Diamond—Transcend

IT'S UP TO YOU!

Your sense of awareness is essential for your rise not only through all levels of the Life Leadership Model, but also through life in general. We have discussed how your intellect is your capacity to perceive reality, an organ or 'eye' with which you see yourself and your interaction with the world. Awareness is what you are able to see and observe using your organs of intellect and consciousness.

Richard L. came to one of my talks not quite expecting the life-changing experience he was going to have. Nor did I. During one of the exercises in awareness, I asked Richard to come on stage and sit himself down next to the other volunteers. The exercise we did with Richard was the one I call, 'BIG YOU, little you'. The aim was to show the audience how there are always two voices in your head, the little cynical, negative voice, what is commonly known as the 'imposter', and the BIG but quiet voice of wisdom.

After Richard finished the exercise and sat back in the audience, his expression was one of amazement. Without prompting, he said a veil had been 'lifted' from his mind. For over 40 years he had been living with the voice of negativity that he had assumed was normal, but now, free from that voice (at least momentarily) he had seen a bigger side to himself that he had not previously been aware. A much bigger side.

Richard had been given a glimpse of self-awareness, which had the power to put to rest the negativity he had lived with for the best part of his life.

LEVELS OF AWARENESS

Black diamond mastery is preparing you for a new way of seeing the world. When you get to this point, you realise what the Life Leadership journey is all about:

Awareness is the key to living a life of abundance and prosperity.

BLACK DIAMOND: TRANSCEND YOUR AWARENESS

Your awareness exists in three distinct levels—body, mind, and spirit. Psychologists label these levels sub-conscious, conscious, and supra-conscious.[43] Like The Diamond Triangle, your sub-conscious, conscious, and supra-conscious form a triangle of awareness, in the centre of which is you.

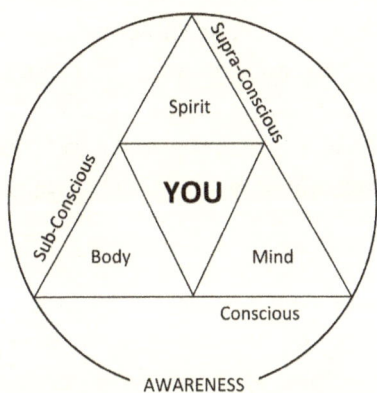

FIGURE 28: The Awareness Triangle—
Supra-Conscious, Conscious, Sub-Conscious

Sub-Conscious

The physical body mostly functions on the lowest level of awareness, the level of sub-consciousness. It has automated processes and functions that run on autopilot, so you can concentrate on other things you need to do throughout the day. These include the digestive system, the cardiovascular system, the respiratory system, the renal system, the immune system, the endocrine system, and the nervous system.

You don't have to think about digesting your food because it's done automatically. So too the blood pumping around your body to and from your heart. You don't have to worry about fighting off the constant attack from viruses, bacteria, and parasites

---

[43] Sigmund Freud, the father of modern psychology, defined his classical model of the human psyche in terms of id, ego and super-ego—the instinctual, logical, and moralistic parts of our consciousness.

because your body's defensive system—your immunity—protects you without you having to give it a second thought. All these things happen at a level of consciousness below your normal consciousness, the sub-conscious state.

Think of your sub-conscious as power without direction. If you think of the main components of a car—engine, steering wheel, accelerator/brake—your sub-conscious is the engine, the power with which you move forward. Without the control of the driver, who steers the vehicle in the intended direction as well as controlling the acceleration, speed, and deceleration, the power of the engine is limited and directionless, even dangerous.

Conscious

The second level of consciousness is that of the mind. This is the normal, everyday state of awareness that occurs during your waking hours. Emotions, and even dreaming, are on this level of consciousness. It's your thoughts, your ideas, your words, your choices, your five senses of sight, sound, taste, touch, and smell. Even pleasure and pain, fear, and love.

This is the level of the mind, the consciousness of thought in which we all function and are all familiar with—the realm of logic and reasoning, art and creativity, belief and religion.

Supra-Conscious

The next level is the supra-consciousness, your highest intelligence. Although this is the highest state of awareness, this is the most neglected level of consciousness. It is often subjugated by the mind and personality to a level even beneath that of the sub-conscious. Yet supra-consciousness is at the level of first cause—the awareness before thought. It is you in your purest state of being.

This is the level of your soul, or human spirit. Because its communication is subtle, its messages often get missed. The distractions of everyday life mean its words are not heard, or they are simply ignored. But sometimes, when its words do get through to our awareness, it comes to us as intuition, insight, inspiration, bliss, sudden knowing, blessedness, awe, and wonder.

It comes in waves of deep peace. The joy of life. The dawning of Goodness, Truth, and Beauty. The awareness of abundance.

SUBJECTIVE AWARENESS

Your triune brain feels distinctly uncomfortable with your supra-consciousness. This level isn't tangible, it can't be captured, measured, or put in a bottle, which your brain needs to identify as something real. This level of consciousness can only be experienced and is therefore reliant upon the observer, you, which makes it subjective.

The subjectiveness of your supra-consciousness, however, gives your rational brain all the ammunition it needs to shoot it down (although it can probably be argued that all levels of consciousness are subjective). From a logical perspective, the human spirit or soul is a purely personal notion. If you think it's there, it's there. If you don't think it's there, it isn't. In other words, like all subjective experiences, the soul is whatever you want it to be. At one end of the scale, this equates to fantasy and delusion, something made up and distinctly unreal. At the other end of the scale, your rational brain will tolerate the idea of the soul, but it certainly isn't scientific or verifiable, and certainly not to be taken seriously.

The body's strength, speed, and internal biological processes can be measured, documented, and verified. That makes it real. The mind's thoughts and mental processes can also be measured, documented, and verified.[44] That also makes it real.

---

[44] Although objective measurement of a person's thoughts is not possible—you can't 'see' someone else's thoughts—the energy associated with thought processes and ongoing brain activity can be measured with instruments such as Magnetic Resonance Imaging (MRI) scanners and electroencephalograph (EEG) monitors.

IT'S UP TO YOU!

Spirit or soul consciousness, however, can't be measured with any known scientific instrumentation. Nor can it be verified. So it isn't real.

That's the logical reasoning of your triune brain and it's a philosophical position many take. Yet this discussion is intended only to offer you a choice: Are you a mind-body-spirit being, or are you simply a mind-body being with no soul, no spirit?

The choice is yours. It's up to you, but whatever you choose, stick to it. Be committed to the truth you hold about yourself.

UNITY CONSCIOUSNESS & HARMONY

It's important to understand how you function on all levels of consciousness. To use the analogy of a chamber orchestra, your spirit or soul is the composer, your mind is the conductor, and your body is the ensemble of musicians. Together they create the music.

The one word that unites composer, conductor, and musicians is harmony. When the composer pens her music, when the conductor organises the musicians into an ensemble, and when each musician knows their role in the ensemble and what they need to play, the result is beautiful music. But what has really been created is *harmony*. Music is the side-effect of that harmony, the physical expression of all three parts of the orchestral process uniting as one.

Music, in this instance, is what harmony sounds like. Music is what harmony feels like. But you can't put harmony in a bottle, measure it, dissect it, or even validate it. Because of its abstract nature,[45] harmony exists beyond the capabilities of scientific instrumentation. It's non-quantifiable.

---

[45] As well as being abstract, harmony, like pregnancy, is also absolute. You can't be a little bit pregnant. You are either pregnant or you're not. Likewise, you can't be a little bit harmonious. You are either in harmony or you're not.

BLACK DIAMOND: TRANSCEND YOUR AWARENESS

What we can measure and validate, however, is its *expression*. Which in this case is beautiful music.

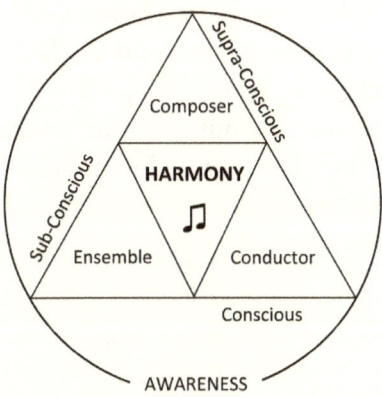

FIGURE 29: The Harmony Triangle—
Composer, Conductor, Ensemble

So it is with consciousness. When all levels of your awareness are in harmony, you too create beautiful music. Harmony occurs when all aspects of your awareness are aligned and functioning as one, as a *unity consciousness*. Only this harmony isn't expressed as orchestral music, it's expressed as the heightened sense of wellbeing:

UNITY CONSCIOUSNESS	
Joy of being alive	Hope and faith
Clarity of thought	Clarity of purpose
Confidence of character	Creativeness and enjoyment
Love for humanity	Passion and enthusiasm

TABLE 27: Unity Consciousness

Harmony consciousness manifests abundance and creates prosperity.

DISUNITY CONSCIOUSNESS & DISHARMONY

The flipside of harmony is disharmony.

Disharmony usually results when one level of consciousness dominates, to the detriment of the others. Most often this is the level of your mind consciousness, the preferred level of your triune brain. When your mind dominates, your awareness gets skewed toward the conscious level, and this disunity of consciousness begins to look like this:

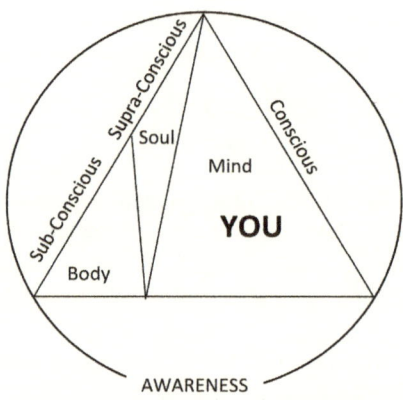

FIGURE 30: Disharmony Consciousness

We know what disharmony sounds like in music, but disharmony in humans is usually expressed as confusion about life and feelings of despair. Other expressions of human disharmony include:

DISUNITY CONSCIOUSNESS	
Hopelessness and futility	Foreboding and fear
Cynicism and despair	Self-Interest and pettiness
Lack of self-worth and belief	Lack of purpose and direction
Powerlessness and lethargy	Heightened negativity

TABLE 28: Disunity Consciousness

BLACK DIAMOND: TRANSCEND YOUR AWARENESS

These examples of disharmony are only meant to highlight the upper end of a spectrum of disharmony, which covers mild to moderate to extreme. Below are some examples of the differences between the disharmony of disunity consciousness and the harmony of unity consciousness.

DISUNITY CONSCIOUSNESS	UNITY CONSCIOUSNESS
Insensitivity and callousness	Compassion and empathy
Closed mindedness	Insight and intuition
Practical realism	Inspiration and creativity
Job for life	Joy of life
Distrust and dejection	Awe and wonder
Perfectionism	Elegance
Mind-Body	Body-Mind-Spirit

TABLE 29:   Disunity Vs Unity Consciouness

We can't always feel on top of the world, however, and always primed to take on the challenges thrown at us; it's simply not human to always be on top of your game, and that's okay. Some days feel worse than others, other days feel better than most. Some days you feel out of sync with everything and everyone, other days you feel nothing can go wrong and everything you touch turns to gold. It's actually more human to be in cyclic rhythms than feeling the same way with the same energy each and every day.

That said, you do have a choice. Do you want your rhythms to occur in the upper end of the spectrum of awareness, or at the lower end? Do you want to vary between higher states of consciousness or between lower states of consciousness?

Your answer will determine your personal brand of success and whether you go some way to achieving mastery.

WATCH HOW YOU SPEAK

Throughout this book we have reiterated that the level of your success depends on how you think. Your thoughts precede your emotions and behaviours, and Life Leaders who have attained black diamond mastery take great care in how they think. Part of this awareness is the vision of themselves as victors, not victims—they see themselves as winners. Most people don't. But if you can't see yourself as a winner, how do propose to perform as a winner?

Part of seeing yourself as a winner, part of seeing yourself crossing the finish line before you've even began, is employing all levels of your awareness to work in harmony so that one level does not dominate at the expense of the others. Just as successful orchestras do. Just as successful sports teams do. They work in unison for a common purpose and vision.

Masters in Life Leadership are therefore very attuned to disharmony. They recognise the symptoms and are quick to treat the cause. Harmony at all times is essential. Life Leaders perform regular self-check-ups to monitor their state of harmony, and they do this by watching how they SPEAK:

- S: Self-Talk
- P: Presence and Mindfulness
- E: Emotional Lingo
- A: Actions and Behaviours
- K: Knee-Jerk Reactions

S: Self-Talk

As often as possible, catch your thoughts and monitor the way you talk to yourself. Are you your best friend or your worst enemy? Are your words positive or negative? Do you lift yourself up, or put yourself down?

Researchers have consistently found that we have a psychological need to belong, and those who have a good social support network are healthier, live longer, and happier than those who don't. But what's even more important is the relationship we have with ourselves. Our thoughts and self-talk greatly affect our wellbeing.

In 1978, Dr. Pauline Clance and Dr. Suzanne Imes introduced the concept of the 'Imposter Syndrome',[46] whereby an individual exhibits a psychological pattern of doubting their abilities and achievements, along with the persistent fear of being exposed as a fraud. The imposter constantly reminds you that you're no good at what you do, that any success you have achieved is either down to luck or the simple result of hard work, which anybody could have done. Either way, your role in your accomplishments is minimised and downplayed.

One way to monitor the presence of the imposter and negative self-talk is to watch how you respond to successes and failures. Do you celebrate little wins, or do you tell yourself you just got lucky? How you think about success and failures affects the chances of future successes.

For instance, if you celebrate the win, the emotional high reinforces the beliefs and actions that led to your success. This triggers the nerve cells in your brain to add another layer of myelination to the neural connections associated with those positive beliefs and actions. The result is a strengthening of all the neural pathways responsible for constructive action, and action, as we know, is vital for success.

Like any persistent negative thought process, however, failing to celebrate your wins and acknowledge your role in achieving success has the opposite effect. Telling yourself you just got lucky only strengthens the neural pathways responsible for unconstructive action, which becomes self-fulfilling.

---

[46] Clance, Pauline R.; Imes, Suzanne A. *The Impostor Phenomenon in High Achieving Women: Dynamics and Therapeutic Intervention*. Psychotherapy Theory, Research and Practice, 1978.

IT'S UP TO YOU!

It really is a case of what you think about you become. Life Leaders therefore watch their self-talk and ensure they celebrate victories and forgive their failures.

P: Presence & Mindfulness

There is a saying that knowledge is power. If this is true, then:

Inner knowledge of self is inner power.

In other words, know thy self and empower thy self.

This is especially important when it comes to controlling your emotional reactions and wellbeing. Which is why mindfulness is so powerful, because when you are more present in the moment you are able to:

1. Increase your self-awareness.
2. Stay focussed for longer.
3. Make better and smarter decisions.

Together this means better results in all the important aspects of your life: health, wealth, relationships, and self-determination.

One of the most powerful tools to increase present moment awareness and mindfulness is meditation. Mindfulness is paying attention to your thoughts, emotions, and body sensations, such as your breath, without passing judgement or reacting to them. When you are mindful, you are present in this moment.

A mind full of thoughts, though, is not mindful. Like a dusty attic crammed with stuff you don't need, your mind has a great capacity to store unnecessary thoughts, emotions, beliefs, and memories. Meditation is like a broom sweeping out the dust and binning all the unwanted items from the mind. Consistent, daily meditation clears the mind, leaving the space empty and pristine for new ideas and inspiration to arise without getting lost in the clutter of mind stuff.

BLACK DIAMOND: TRANSCEND YOUR AWARENESS

As the Buddhists say, you should do half an hour of meditation a day. Unless, of course, you're really busy. Then you should do an hour.

There are currently thousands of studies that show the benefits of meditation upon your physical body and state of mind, such as anxiety and depression, irritable bowel syndrome (IBS), chronic pain, addictions, even tinnitus. Meditation also improves your health by boosting your body's immunity and ability to fight infection.

What the research reveals is that meditation and mindfulness increase your ability to recruit higher brain functionality to minimise or regulate lower brain functionality. It does this by creating a conscious space for your higher self to enter into your sphere of awareness. This strengthens self-compassion, increasing your ability to be kind to yourself and be less judgmental, and thus provides an antidote to the negative self-talk of the 'imposter'.

The table below highlights the main research findings of meditation and mindfulness on the brain.

PHYSICAL EFFECTS	SYMPTOMATIC BENEFIT
Increased cortical thickness and grey matter of the brain	Improved memory Emotional stability Heightened sensory perception Increased self-regulation
Reduction of Amygdala (Limbic System)	Less reactive, more responsive
Increased thickening of prefrontal cortex	Improved Pain regulation Emotional regulation Better processing of distraction and conflict

TABLE 30: Meditation and Mindfulness Effects and Benefits

IT'S UP TO YOU!

Mindfulness is essentially the practice of present moment awareness, and meditation is one of the best techniques to achieve mindfulness. In this regard, your body is the gateway to being present in this moment of now. Your mind is usually not present. It is usually thinking of what's happened in the past, or what's going to happen in the future. But your body is always present because it's always 'here'. For this reason, many mindfulness techniques focus on 'feeling' your body, such as your breath, chakra areas, or touch sensations. The intention is to stop your mind wandering in the past and future and bring it into the present moment.

An example of this is happiness and joy. Happiness in the past is a state of nostalgia. Happiness in the future is a state of anticipation and excitement. They are mental abstractions—virtual, but not real experiences. But happiness in this present moment is the feeling of joy and bliss, which are higher states of being because they are 'real time' or 'now' experiences of the fullness of life. Imagine living a life of permanent bliss?

This is the power of presence and mindfulness.

E: Emotional Lingo

We have covered much of this in our discussion on the happiness formula ($H = S + C + V$) in Chapter 5, where the biggest impact you can make on your sense of wellbeing is the voluntary thoughts and choices you make.

Part of your voluntary thoughts and choices is the emotional lingo you use. Life Leaders ascending to mastery deliberately watch the words that come out of their mouth when speaking to others. They are alert to their state of emotion.

Let's use the common example of meeting and greeting someone. When they ask how you are, how do respond? Do you say, 'Oh, okay, I guess,' or, 'Not too bad.'

Notice, though, the emotional lingo in these responses. They border on suppressed or downbeat. At best they are neutral.

But if it's true that what you think about you experience, then what you talk about you feel. If you speak in a downbeat or neutral manner, then this is going to trigger the emotions you are most likely going to feel. So when someone greets you and asks how you are, even if you're not feeling your best, why not use upbeat emotional lingo, like, 'I'm great! Thanks for asking.' Or, if that's a step too far, 'I'm feeling pretty good.'

What you feel is what you attract. This is because your body 'feels' and your body, as just discussed, is present in this moment of now.

So use your emotional lingo to your advantage.

A: Actions & Behaviours

As a Life Leader, your actions and behaviours should align with your values and reflect the character you are building.

If you value health and wellbeing, then your behaviour should reflect this. This includes a fitness regime, eating nutritionally, minimising caffeine and alcohol, and regular rest. The test will come when faced with a pizza or donut. What do you value more, your taste buds or the vision of your healthy self?

An affirmation you might use in such instances can be: 'I value a healthy me over and above all else that is happening right now.'

If you value peace of mind, then your behaviour should reflect this. This includes mindfulness practices, increased alertness, minimising emotional conflicts, and an attitude of calmness. The test will come when conflict arises in the family or at work. What do you value more, being right or the vision of your peaceful self?

An affirmation you might use in this instance can be: 'I value peace of mind, theirs and mine, over and above all else that is happening right now.'

Life Leaders are mindful of their actions and behaviours.

K: Kneejerk Reactions

The way a Life Leader responds to their immediate circumstances separates them from the crowd. A Life Leader responds consciously, others react unconsciously.

When a doctor taps a patient's kneecap with a patella hammer, she is observing the reflexive kick of the lower leg. When the patella is tapped, nerve cells send a signal up to the spinal cord. Some of the signal travels all the way up the spine to the brain, registering as touch or pain. However, most of the signal rebounds straight back down to the leg muscles, bypassing the brain and causing the leg to jerk. This is why it feels like the leg kicks on its own accord, because the brain hasn't been in control of the action.

Sometimes it can seem as if we react to circumstances in a reflexive manner, without thought. It's as if the brain has been bypassed. We say things we shouldn't have said and behave in a way we shouldn't have behaved.

Life Leaders know they always have time to respond in a deliberate and considered way. They don't rush to speak or act without thought. They take on board Victor Frankl's advice, that between stimulus and response there is a gap, and in that gap is your power to choose your response.

Because in your response lies your growth and freedom.

This is Life Leadership mastery.

BLACK DIAMOND: TRANSCEND YOUR AWARENESS

BLACK DIAMOND PRACTICE—STANDING TO ATTENTION

The exercise for black diamond level is to transcend your awareness so that you can rejuvenate your Inner Power and cross the finishing line to Life Leadership mastery. I call this exercise, 'Standing to Attention,' like a soldier standing on parade.

There are three parts to this exercise, designed to help you focus on your three levels of consciousness—mind, body, and spirit—and bypass the self-limiting effects of your triune brain:

1. Watch Your Inner World
2. Listen to Your Words
3. Observe Your Behaviours

<u>Watch Your Inner World</u>

Watching your inner world involves the continual awareness of your thoughts, beliefs, mottos, and emotions. It means being alert, not sleepy. It means being mindful of how your thoughts trigger your emotions, particularly stress, and how your beliefs filter your perception of the world around you.

This is especially important if you find yourself slipping into disharmony and negativity. A good exercise to shake off the drowsiness and build alertness of your thoughts is the 'What Were You Thinking?' exercise:

-> Observe your current or present thought or emotion.
-> What were you thinking before that thought/emotion? In other words, what thought lead to your current thought/emotion?
-> Next, what preceded that thought/emotion?
-> Then, what preceded that thought/emotion?

The aim is to trace back your thought chain as far as you can. A good beginning is four or five, but with practice you might even be able to go back ten preceding thoughts.

This way, you can break the chain of any negative or self-defeating thought process and prevent it spiralling into self-sabotaging emotions and behaviours. But only as long as you stay attentive and watch your inner world.

Listen to Your Words

The second part of Standing to Attention is listening to the words you speak. Just as you must remain alert to your thoughts, you must also be attentive to what you say. It requires you to recognise how your words represent your thoughts, which in turn influence your behaviours.

Take particular notice of the words that are self-limiting, excuse making, or disempowering:

- I Can't. I Won't. I Ain't.
- Shouldn't. Couldn't.
- I don't have...
- Why me?
- It's not my fault.
- I can't live without it.

These types of words are red flags to the self-limiting thoughts and beliefs that underpin them. But this is where the 'Power of the Yeti' enters the fray, and you can use its power in a very simple way.

Whenever you catch yourself using self-limiting words and phrases, such as 'I can't' or 'I shouldn't have', the simplest and most powerful way to turn the negativity of those words into a positive, empowering statement is by inserting the conjunction *'yet'* immediately afterwards. For instance, if you hear yourself saying, 'I'm not clever enough to do that,' immediately put a 'yet' at the end of the sentence, like this: 'I'm not clever enough to do that... *yet*.'

The next step is to add a pro-active statement that nullifies the original statement and motivates you to act in a self-empowering way. An example would be: 'I'm not clever enough to do that... *yet*, but I will be when I train myself how to do it.'

Here are some other examples of the Power of the Yeti:

- -> 'I don't have the time for that... *yet*, but I will make sure I create time for it.'
- -> 'It's not my fault I was late for work... *yet* if I leave a little bit earlier tomorrow, I will arrive on time.'
- -> 'Why do I always have bad luck?... *yet* I'm sure that's the end of it and my luck is about to change.'

You can turn any negative or self-defeating statement into a positive, affirming statement. But only as long as you are attentive and listen to your words.

Observe Your Behaviours

The third part of Standing to Attention is observing your behaviours. Take particular notice of any behaviours that are self-limiting, knee-jerk, or self-sabotaging.

The practice of detachment will assist you in observing your behaviour. Sometimes when you dream, you see through your own eyes as you do in the waking day, which is known as first-person observation. At other times, you might dream as if you are watching yourself from above or out of your body, which is known as third-person observation.

This third-person detachment is also like watching yourself on video or in front of a mirror. Professional speakers often watch a video recording of their speech with the volume muted. The intent is to watch their body language, the little twitches, shuffles, scratches, and facial expressions they weren't aware of during the presentation. Ballet dancers and stage actors often rehearse in front of a mirror for exactly the same reason—to catch any unintended gestures or movements that they are unaware of and to ensure their performance is as polished as they can make it.

It's therefore good practice to observe your actions and behaviours in the third-person. This requires strong concentration and mindfulness, being fully attentive of what your body is doing in the present moment. When you observe your behaviours in everyday activities, also take note of the motives behind those actions. This will help to root out any sub-conscious patterns and blockages that you might not be aware of.

One exercise that builds your self-observation skills is eating. In our busy lifestyle, Westerners are often guilty of scoffing down their meal as quickly as possible, swallowing their food without properly chewing. Our minds are usually on the conversation we're having at the dinner table, or the list of things we need to do, and rarely on the act of chewing. But failure to properly chew our meal forces our stomach and bowels to do more work to digest the food than they were designed to do, which could explain a lot of modern-day digestive tract illnesses.

Proper chewing—which is simply chewing slowly until the food has turned to liquid in your mouth—not only reduces the load on your lower digestive system, but it also builds self-observation and attentiveness, which is akin to mindfulness. This is an easy exercise to do at every mealtime.

You can eliminate any self-sabotaging behaviour and prevent them from recurring. But only as long as you are attentive and observe your behaviours.

PART 5

LIFE LEADERSHIP
PRACTICES

TIER #3: ELITE

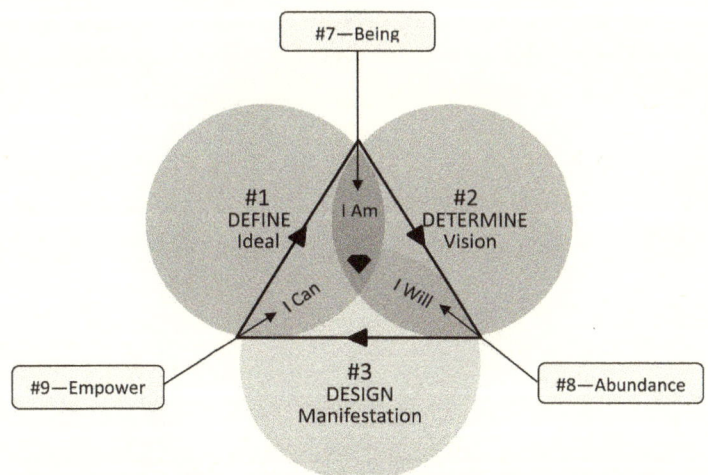

14 GREEN DIAMOND: YOUR NATURAL STATE OF BEING

LIFE LEADERSHIP PRACTICE #7

THE NEXT LEVEL of your Life Leadership journey is green diamond. The aim of this level is to attain elite-level knowledge of Life Skill #3–What, and progress to white diamond level within 3-4 months. The practice of knowing your natural state of being is the third in the process of 'Reconnecting' and moving into Quadrant #1 in the Empowered Living Index.

The core of this Life Leadership Practice is to understand the essence of who you are. In The Diamond Triangle, your natural state of being is the final building block in your 'I Am' axis, and is now looking like this:

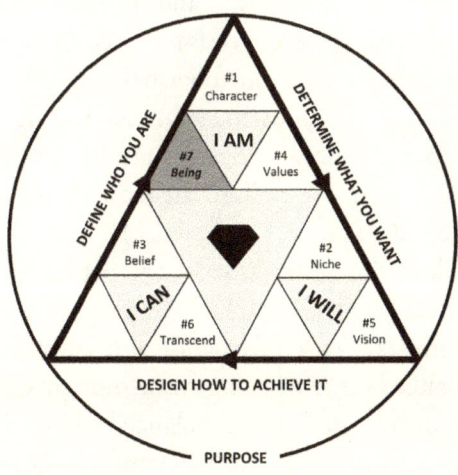

FIGURE 31:   Green Diamond—Being

YOUR LIFE FORCE

Your three levels of awareness lead to something of immense importance—your sense of being.

This is the sense of who, what, where, when, and even how, you are as a unique individual here on earth—who you are in your core.

But this is something contemporary culture has lost sight of. Indigenous cultures, such as the Native American Indians and the Australian Aborigines, have not. Since time immemorial, indigenous people have made no distinction between the land and themselves, between nature and humanity. They believe everything is imbued with life—the trees, the animals, the earth, the wind, the water, humans. Nature is part of them and they are part of nature. We come from the earth and we are part of the earth. What harms one harms the other because there is no 'me' and no 'it', just different forms of the one thing called nature. It therefore stands to reason that harmony and balance with nature is vital to these cultures.

But as human culture evolved, that connection with nature was diluted and eventually lost, at least in Western society. We've forgotten where we're from. Our origins are a foggy memory. As a culture, we've become so removed and disconnected from nature that it is not only a foreign entity, it is now a commodity, something to consume and exploit for our own benefit. We are destroying rainforests, the lungs of our earth, at an accelerating pace. We have almost fished out the oceans. Species are becoming extinct at a rate never before seen. We pollute the land, skies, and seas on an industrial scale. Life is cheap.

But what does the destruction of the planet have to do with your sense of being?

First, it signifies a lack of balance and harmony. When you have an unbalanced sense of being, your thoughts, emotions, and behaviour are unbalanced. An unbalanced sense of being means you identify only in what you want, in your own desires and needs, which leads to self-centredness and ultimately self-destructiveness.

GREEN DIAMOND: YOUR NATURAL STATE OF BEING

On a grand scale, when seven billion humans act this way, it can only lead to one thing—the accelerating destruction of the planet's resources, its fauna and flora, and even humanity itself.

Second, the destruction of the planet signifies an incompletion within us. This ties in with being unbalanced. A car with one of its wheels missing, for instance, is going to be incomplete and unbalanced. It may still be able to function to some degree, but not very well. So too with human beings. When you identify only with your mind, body, and emotions, something is missing. You're therefore going to be incomplete and unbalanced, even dysfunctional.

That missing piece, of course, is your spirit. Your life force.

Your life force is the energy that fuels and replenishes your mind, body, and emotions. You know when that life force is absent or removed because the mind and body die at that point. Yet although it can't be measured in a laboratory, it doesn't mean your life force isn't real.

So here's another flow of logic to consider:

- -> Your body is currently alive, which you can measure and document. You can take this as a scientific and verifiable fact.
- -> Yet a dead corpse can also be measured and documented, a scientific and verifiable fact. What, then, is the missing factor between a dead body and a live body? What essence is keeping your body and mind functioning right now? What life force has left the dead body?
- -> Can this 'aliveness' or life force be bottled, measured, and documented?
- -> Can we locate this life force somewhere in your body? Is it somewhere in your mind? Is it located elsewhere, perhaps not even in your body?

IT'S UP TO YOU!

For good or for bad, this life force cannot be captured and inserted into a test tube to undergo rigorous scientific experimentation. It's unquantifiable. Dissect your body with a scalpel to its last molecule and you won't find it. Your life force sustains you, yet it is more than the energy you derive from eating food and drinking water.

It is more than just calories and kilojoules.

YOUR EXPERIENCE OF BEING

Although your life force can't be measured with scientific instruments, it can be *felt*. It's not something to be located and found, only *experienced*, like harmonious music. In its purest form, your life force can be felt as your natural state of joy, security, acceptance, peace, and freedom.[47]

Children know this instinctively. They express their natural state freely and without hindrance. Their life force radiates like an aura. Visit any kindergarten and see for yourself. Children feel naturally happy, safe, valued, peaceful, and free. They run, they laugh, they squeal with delight. They fly through the day as if there's no tomorrow. Until the pain comes, or the violation, the hunger, the deprivation, the abuse. Until society tells them to grow up, that life isn't all peaches and roses, that there's a real world out there and they must prepare for it. Then it's buried, sometimes forever.

But it's never lost. It never leaves. Even on the cloudiest days and darkest nights, the sun is still there. Even when it rains, the sun remains. Similarly, your natural state of being is always there. Even in your darkest hours, it's always available. Its light might be hard to see, but as long as you're alive your natural state of being remains the core of who you are. You can find it again, that lost innocence. You can find that joy of life you once had as a child.

---

[47] Readers can read more in my book *Your Natural State of Being*, DoctorZed Publishing, 2012.

But how do you experience more joy, more security, more appreciation, more peace, more freedom? How do you experience more of your true self? How do you reconnect with your human spirit?

Through choice.

YOUR NATURAL CHOICE

It's natural to want to feel happier, safer, more appreciated, more peaceful, and freer. It's a normal human condition to want these things and to want them all the time.

Invariably, these are the things we hope money can buy. Or even the things we'll gain from a new job, a new partner, a new house, travel. Ask yourself why you want to earn more money or win the lottery, or why you're looking for a new career path, or why you have your eye out for another partner. The answer will probably be a combination of happiness, security, belonging, peace, and freedom.

What gets in the way and blocks the experience of these things, however, is the way you think. Or more precisely, a paucity mindset. The unyielding belief that you don't have enough of what you want, which is the direct opposite of an abundance mindset, triggers the act of seeking whomever or whatever will give you what you want. Usually money, a partner, a job, a house, or a different location.

If this seems familiar, the good news is that *you already have what you're looking for.*

You don't need more money. You don't need a new job or partner. You don't need to travel afar. What you're looking for is already inside you. In fact, it *is* you. Your natural state of being is who you really are—your natural state of *abundance*. You are not the sadness, the insecurities, the unworthiness, the anxiety, the failings. These negativities happen in the everyday cycle of life, but that doesn't make them who you are. Who you are is abundant.

IT'S UP TO YOU!

Who you are is BIG. So it really is a natural choice to want more of yourself.

The question is, then: *How* do I get more of myself?

The answer, of course, is by choosing more.

You get more of yourself by choosing more of yourself.

That's your free will—your freedom to choose who you are. That means who you are is a choice. The great news is, you get to decide who you are and what you want to experience about yourself. Ask and you shall receive:

-> Want more joy, more happiness?
Then choose it.

-> Want more safety, more security?
Then choose it.

-> Want more acceptance, more respect?
Then choose it.

-> Want more peace, more serenity?
Then choose it.

-> Want more freedom, more self-determination?
Then choose it.

Make a decision. Take action. Ask more of yourself. That's your power.

Will it happen overnight? Will you get more of what you want immediately by simply choosing it?

Probably not, but just as a mighty oak grows from a single acorn, choosing your natural state of being is a growth process. Little by little, day after day, week after week, the continual act of choosing who you really are over who you are *not* nurtures that seed within you, that life force, until it grows so big it becomes who you are in everything you think, feel, and do.

GREEN DIAMOND: YOUR NATURAL STATE OF BEING

Your natural state of being is not something you get, it's something you already are. It develops and matures from the inside. So let your sense of being be rooted in the things you want more of—joy, security, acceptance, peace, and freedom. Don't chase these things in material things, other people, other places, for they are impermanent and fleeting. They never last.

Rather, cultivate these things within you and reap the fruits of your growth.

Because the fruits of tomorrow are in the seeds of today.

YOUR 'I AM'

We have now completed the first axis, 'I Am', on your Life Leadership journey.

We have discussed the importance of building your 'I Am' through defining your character, values, and being—your who, why, and what. Your character is what makes your 'I Am' great. It's what defines you in the eyes of others. It is the cornerstone upon which you build the biggest and best version of yourself.

Life Leaders are great characters. They make a great success of their lives in whatever they decide to do and in whatever field they work, whether they are homemakers, teachers, politicians, athletes, accountants, engineers, scientists, artists, or entrepreneurs. Great characters know that it doesn't matter what they do, it matters who they are—and who they are is a choice. Great characters make that choice. Life leaders make that choice.

Your values are the principles and standards by which you measure yourself. They are the things you stand for and believe in on a personal and community level. The Core Values of Goodness, Truth and Beauty are the seed from which all personal and community values arise. The extent to which you commit to your Core Values determines the extent to which you master Life Leadership.

IT'S UP TO YOU!

Your being is a synergy of mind, body, and spirit. Like the composer, conductor, and musicians in an orchestra, when your sub-conscious, conscious, and supra-conscious work in harmony, the result is beautiful music. Although subjective and unquantifiable, this harmony is experienced as a deep and permanent sense of joy, security, acceptance, peace, and freedom—your natural state of being. Your true self.

Your character, values, and being define who you are. They are your 'I Am'.

GREEN DIAMOND PRACTICE—YOUR NATURAL STATE OF VALUES

There are two main sources of knowledge: knowledge that comes through learning—theoretical—and knowledge that comes through experience—empirical. Most of our education is based on learning the theory of something, then applying that theory in practice. First you learn *what* you need to know, then you learn *how* to apply it.

The Life Leadership Practice for green diamond, *#7 Your Natural State of Being*, will therefore focus on the first type of knowledge, theoretical. The practice for the next level at white diamond, *#8 The Attitudes of Abundant Living*, will focus on the second type, empirical. The aim is to gain theoretical and empirical knowledge of your natural state of being.

In *Table 31: Your Natural State of Values*, the list of values from The Value Pack in Chapter 11 have been rearranged to align with your five natural states of being: Joy, Security, Acceptance, Peace, and Freedom.

All values pare down to one of five natural states of being. For instance, if one of your values is humour or leisure, it aligns with your natural state of joy. If one of your values is power or intellect, it aligns with your natural state of security. You will also note the obvious anomaly in the table: love. Love is the universal human value. It transcends all other values and is, in fact, the source of Goodness, Truth and Beauty and thereby the root of all our values and natural states of being.

You know this to be true in your own experience. Recall the time when you first fell in love. Were you not overtly happy and joyful? Did you not feel safe and secure with that person? Did they not accept you completely for who you are, and you of them? Did you not feel totally at peace, unaffected by whatever else was happening around you? Did you not feel utterly free and

IT'S UP TO YOU!

a lightness of being, as if your feet didn't touch the ground when you walked?

That's what love does—it removes all your inner barriers to experiencing your true self.

JOY	SECURITY	ACCEPTANCE	PEACE	FREEDOM
Happiness	Autonomy	Meaning	Mindfulness	Adventure
Creativity	Safety	Privacy	Serenity	Change
Excitement	Health	Self-respect	Religion	Creativity
Beauty	Education	Belonging	Mastery	Variety
Leisure	Structure	Status	Collaboration	Liberty
Wellbeing	Cooperation	Achievement	Wisdom	Equality
Fun	Power	Fame	Forgiveness	Democracy
Mastery	Status	Influence	Harmony	Diversity
Pleasure	Wealth	Prestige	Balance	Openness
Gratitude	Financial Gain	Reputation	Nature	Truth
Challenge	Productivity	Community	Spirituality	Personal Expression
Humour	Advancement	Loyalty	Quality	Honesty
Philanthropy	Location	Teamwork	Legacy	Mercy
Goodness	Stability	Recognition	Competence	Fairness
Curiosity	Knowledge	Friendship	Communication	Leadership
Arts	Intellect	Merit	Patience	Innovation
Love	Love	Love	Love	Love

TABLE 31: Your Natural State of Values

GREEN DIAMOND: YOUR NATURAL STATE OF BEING

***

The exercise now is to follow these steps:

- -> Locate the 7 values in the Value Pack that you identified as your top 7 values in the practice for blue diamond and circle them. (You are permitted to circle a column category, such as Freedom, if that was one of your identified values.)
- -> Total which column has most values circled. (A column category is worth 2x other values.)
- -> The column with the most circled values represents that part of your natural state of being you most want to connect and align with.

For instance, if you have two or more values circled in the acceptance column, your focus will be on how to experience more self-acceptance. If you have two or more values circled in the freedom column, your focus will be on how to experience more of your unlimited natural freedom.

Now that you have identified your area of focus, the next Life Practice, *#8 The Attitudes of Abundant Living*, will teach you how to experience more of what you want.

15 WHITE DIAMOND: THE ATTITUDES OF ABUNDANT LIVING

LIFE LEADERSHIP PRACTICE #8

THE NEXT LEVEL of your Life Leadership journey is white diamond. The aim of this level is to attain elite-level knowledge of Life Skill #4–How, and progress to purple diamond level within 3-4 months. The practice of abundant living is the third in the process of 'Realigning' and moving into Quadrant #1 in the Empowered Living Index.

The core of this Life Leadership Practice is knowing how to express your natural state of being. In The Diamond Triangle, abundant living is the final building block in your 'I Will' axis, and is now looking like this:

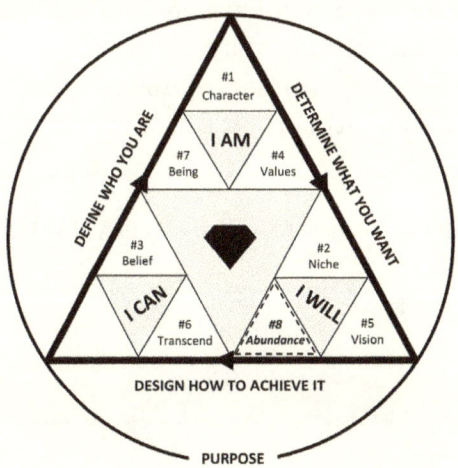

FIGURE 32: White Diamond—Abundance

There are three Life Leadership attitudes that can help you make a positive change to your life and the lives of those you care about. I call these *The Attitudes of Abundant Living*. Used consistently, these attitudes not only help you develop a strong character and affirming values, they also open the door to experiencing the abundance of your natural state of being.

John Amatt was the leader of Canada's first successful expedition to the summit of Mt Everest. He used his experience of conquering the world's highest mountain as a metaphor for the mountains we face through the challenges of everyday life:

> *Adventure isn't hanging on a rope on the side of a mountain. Adventure is an attitude that we must apply to the day-to-day obstacles of life—facing new challenges, seizing new opportunities, testing our resources against the unknown and, in the process, discovering our own unique potential.*[48]

Part of discovering your own unique potential and inner power is unveiling the limitlessness essence at the core of your being, the life force you once knew and revelled in as a child. Part of the 'adventurous attitude' you need to apply to the day-to-day obstacles in life are The Attitudes of Abundant Living. Like the 3 Golden Rules, these attitudes are concise and easy to remember:

THE ATTITUDES OF ABUNDANT LIVING:

#1: *Giving*
#2: *Forgiving*
#3: *Thanksgiving*

---

[48] John Amatt, *Straight to the Top and Beyond: Nine Keys for Meeting the Challenge of Changing Times*, CDG Books, Canada, 1995

WHITE DIAMOND: THE ATTITUDES OF ABUNDANT LIVING

Life rewards you for who you are and what you do. Therefore give abundantly, forgive abundantly, and give thanks abundantly to experience your true inner state of abundance.

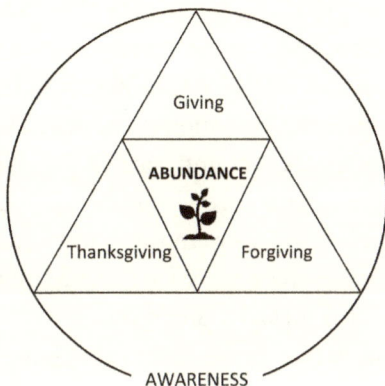

FIGURE 33: The Attitudes of Abundant Living

An easy way to remember is: *Thanks For Giving!*

GIVING

The attitude of giving is the attitude of generosity. The attitude of service. The attitude of charity. The attitude of value. The attitude of kindness. The attitude of sacrifice.

Life is mysterious, as we know, and one of its mysteries is this:

The more you give, the more you receive.

This is because Life is a mirror.

Life reflects everything back to you in one form or another, equally and in the same measure in accordance with the Law of Thermodynamics. On a practical level, this means what you put in, you get back. Put garbage in, get garbage out. Put goodness in, get goodness out. Similar to karma, what is in play is The Law of Reflection. Your experience of the world is but a *reflection* of who you are at all levels of awareness—mind, body, spirit. You are not an unwitting pawn in the Game of Life. You are simply being reflected back to yourself.

This doesn't imply that if you give thousands of dollars to charity you'll receive even more from an unexpected windfall. That's not how the Law of Reflection works. What you receive in return for your generosity isn't money or financial gain. What you receive—what is *reflected* straight back at you—is something far more important than money: your natural state of being.

What you receive is more joy, more security, more appreciation, more peace, and more freedom. More of what everyone wants—more abundance. This means more of *you*.

Here then is the secret to the attitude of giving:

The act of giving reveals more of your true self.

This is why service to your community is so important. This is why generosity to others is so important. The act of giving reflects more of who you really are.

But the converse is also true. Hold back on giving, cease being generous to others, short-change your value and worth, and what is revealed isn't more of your natural state of being but more of your triune brain.

You can't give what you don't have, but you can certainly be generous with what you do have; and when you give, give without the need for anything in return. Give for giving's sake.

Table 32: The Attitude of Giving lists some things besides money you already have that you can give in abundance. There are four guidelines for optimal giving:

1. Give without Recognition—forego the need to be credited for your generosity.
2. Give without Impatience—be patient in how the recipient of your generosity uses your gift.

3. Give without Condition—give unconditionally and allow your gift to be used as the receiver needs, not how you want it to be used.
4. Give without Expectation—be generous without the need to be recompensed and expect nothing in return.

THE ATTITUDE OF GIVING	
Your time	Your presence
Your kindness	Your understanding
Your smile	Your appreciation
Your patience	Your interest
Your wisdom	Your blessing
Your help	Your forgiveness
Your attention	Your gratitude

TABLE 32:   The Attitude of Giving

There is a way to receiving more of what you want for yourself too, by using the Law of Reflection to your advantage. Although it might appear counterintuitive, this is it:

Give unto others that which you wish for yourself.

People, for instance, like to feel important. Acceptance is one of the fundamental needs of humanity. They want to feel appreciated. They want to feel a sense of significance. They want to feel indispensable. They want to feel needed. Therefore, give people what they want. Show interest in them and what they do. Give them your time. Make them feel important and appreciated. Make them feel needed and wanted.

The wonderful thing is, you too will feel important. You too will feel needed and wanted. You too will feel appreciated. In fact, you will experience one of the great blessings in life: you will feel as though you have made a significant impact for good in somebody else's life.

This is the Law of Reflection at work, and it also applies to happiness, security, peace, and freedom. Make somebody else happy and you'll feel happy. Make somebody feel safe and secure and you'll feel safe and secure. Make someone feel at ease and at peace and you'll feel at ease and at peace. Help uplift somebody and liberate them from whatever is holding them back and you'll feel uplifted and liberated.

You already have these things in abundance. In fact, they're limitless. They are never-ending. So give abundantly. You have more than you'll ever need for yourself. But should you feel the need for more of these things, you now know what to do—give them away.

For what you give you shall receive.

FORGIVING

The attitude of forgiving is the attitude of compassion. The attitude of tolerance. The attitude of mercy. The attitude of understanding. The attitude of healing. The attitude of freedom.

The act of forgiveness is a characteristic of Life Leadership. Your triune brain just won't do it; it's simply not in its nature. But, just as giving to others reveals more of your true self and returns to you in abundance that which you give, the attitude of forgiveness is also self-revealing:

> *Forgiveness removes the blockages and obstacles to accessing your abundance.*

The degree to which you experience your natural state of being is proportional to the degree to which you are prepared to forgive. At worst, the lack of forgiveness for something that has happened in the past steals the joy of life you feel in the present moment. It also steals your sense of self-worth, your inner peace, your sense of freedom.

On a lesser scale, the lack of forgiveness can lead to a general sense of unease and disquiet. But unease unchecked over time can turn into to dis-ease. This is because any blockage or obstacle that prevents the full expression of your natural state of being can cause stress, and too much stress over time is potentially harmful to your health.

On the other hand, anything that can remove the blockage, or bypass the obstacle, liberates the experience of your true self, which reduces stress and is therefore beneficial to your state of health. Forgiveness is an act of self-healing. To forgive someone or something for a wrong done unto you is cathartic. Not for others, but for yourself. The best reason to forgive is to heal your wounds and move on. It's a self-empowering act.

Forgiveness allows you to say, 'What's done is done. It was bad. It wasn't nice. I'm hurting. But you're forgiven and I can now heal my wounds and move on with my life.'

Sometimes you also need to forgive yourself for the hurt you've caused others. When you hang onto past wrongs you've committed, you get mired in guilt and remorse and can't move on. This happens when the past is remembered and replayed— physically, emotionally, psychologically. Although a wrong may have been done by you or to you, you relive it every time you think about it, every time you replay it in your mind. You relive it every time you *reflect* on it.

When you look back at the grievance and relive it, that memory is a reflection of yourself from the past, a kind of virtual reality that is replayed and re-experienced in the present moment. Your past self literally haunts you, and the stress evoked from the memory is just as powerful and real as the stress evoked from the actual incident you are recalling.

Unfortunately, reliving a past wrong keeps the mental and emotional wounds raw and open, preventing them from healing. Yet forgiveness of the wrongdoer, whether it's yourself or another, anaesthetises the memory so that its pain is no longer felt. Forgiveness doesn't make you forget what has happened, but it does reduce the pain and suffering that the memory can cause. Without the distraction of pain and hurt, you can then learn the lessons of the past without feeling as though the past is always repeating itself.

What's the point in punishing yourself now or in the future for mistakes made in the past? Forgiveness gives you the space to learn the lessons of the mistake, grow from it, and then let it go. Forgiveness of self is therefore an important ingredient of self-compassion. This isn't being selfish, rather the opposite. It's being kind, gentle, and having understanding of yourself. Self-compassion is the path toward improved mental health and greater life satisfaction.

Forgiveness is how you bypass your emotional midbrain, which wants to keep feeling the hurt, to keep feeling the pain. Because then it can relive over and over again the injustice done to it and continue as a victim. It blames. It rants. It raves. It demands immediate justice, no matter how small the perceived wrong. That's why it won't forgive under any circumstance.

Your supra-consciousness, though, wants you to heal and move on. It knows there's no point in maintaining a sense of victimisation, no matter how bad the wrong, because it knows that victimisation prevents healing and stunts growth. Which is the antithesis of what you really are—limitless, unending, continual growth.

This is the main reason to forgive. Whereas unhealed wounds cause you to relive past hurts again and again, forgiveness allows these same wounds to heal and free your attention to the present moment, where the fullness of Life is.

And where the fullness of Life is, so is the fullness and abundance of your natural state of being.

THANKSGIVING

The attitude of thanksgiving is the attitude of gratitude. The attitude of appreciation. The attitude of humility. The attitude of respect. The attitude of fulfillment.

Of the three Attitudes of Abundant Living, gratitude is perhaps the easiest to implement. There's always something to be grateful for. You just have to look for it. If you're stuck for gratitude, at the very least you can be grateful to nature for producing the air you breathe.

As with giving and forgiving, the act of giving thanks to something or someone other than yourself also reveals more of your inner nature. One of the wonderful side-effects of gratitude is that it multiplies. The more grateful you are, the more Goodness, Truth and Beauty you see. You feel as though you have more of the good things in life. You feel abundant. It does this because of one simple reason:

The act of giving thanks unlocks the joy of life.

Gratitude is a game-changer. There is a direct relationship between your happiness and how grateful you are. Gratitude can be considered an investment in your long-term happiness—the more you give thanks, the happier you become. Positive psychologists have even put a figure on how much happier you become. The simple act of saying 'Thanks!' regularly and practicing grateful thinking has been shown to improve your happiness by as much as 25%.[49] People who express gratitude are happier than those who don't. They have a deeper, longer lasting joyful mood.

---

[49] Robert A. Emmons PhD, *Thanks!: How the New Science of Gratitude Can Make You Happier*, Houghton Mifflin Harcourt, 2007.

IT'S UP TO YOU!

In the happiness equation ($H = S + C + V$), gratitude is a voluntary choice you make, and this has maximum impact on your sense of wellbeing. It sounds simple, but that's how it works.

In fact, the Law of Reflection is in action again. As long as your gratitude is sincere, and your humility is genuine, regular deposits of thanksgiving will ensure your happiness and joy will grow just as any money saved in a bank account grows with regular cash deposits. Although nothing is guaranteed in life (except death and taxes, as they say), gratitude is a 99.9% guarantee of securing your future joy.

As the motto goes, happiness doesn't come from having everything you want, it comes from wanting everything you have. Being grateful increases your want for what you already have. Therefore, the happiest people in life are the people who are most grateful for what they have.

The attitude of gratitude is very powerful. There is potency in wanting and appreciating what you have, rather than taking it for granted and hoping for something else. If you focus on what you don't have, negativity and discontent results. This is exactly what your triune brain does. If you allow it, it will process the world around you through the filter of victimisation. Your thoughts, emotions, and instincts will focus on what you don't have, what is missing in this very moment. You will focus on the problem, not the solution. You will see the glass as half empty.

This eventually spills over as a continual state of moaning, complaining, dissatisfaction, and ingratitude. You will resist your current situation. You will be dissatisfied with where you are and even with those who you're with. You will begin to dislike yourself.

This is why giving thanks is so important. It refocusses your attention on what you do have in this very moment, to take pleasure in the little things, to count your blessings. To focus on the glass half full is to have an abundance attitude. It is to be solution driven and not problem fixated. This state of mind cannot help but be anything other than joyous and generous.

Life Leaders use the Law of Reflection to mirror what they would like to receive. Being grateful for what you have naturally reflects the positivity in your life-situation; and when your positivity is reflected, it gets enhanced, it gets magnified. You then begin to feel that not only are you lucky, you are blessed.

One such blessing is a greater appreciation of your life-situation—the person you have become, the work you do, the relationships you have, the life you live—and when you appreciate more of who you are and what you already have, it will seem you already have more of what you have.

Appreciation appreciates.

RECEIVING

There is a fourth attitude as important and powerful as the first three—the Attitude of Receiving.

The Game of Life is a wonderful game of giving and receiving. It is a two-way process. Not only are they noble and honourable, giving, forgiving, and thanksgiving are advantageous to your success and prosperity. However, if you cannot receive the success and prosperity that comes your way with as much openness and generosity as you give, then these gifts will fall on barren soil. They will not find nurture in you, and they will not flourish. Like something that has been ignored, they will eventually wither and be lost to you.

What you sow you reap. But if you cannot receive well, all your good efforts of giving, forgiving, and thanksgiving will not be maximised. Your success and prosperity will be as limited as much as your ability to receive the gifts of your efforts.

There are two types of receiving, passive and active:

1. Passive: where you accept with gratitude what comes to you without effort on your behalf.
2. Active: where your specific actions open the door to opportunity, and you receive what you set out to get.

I only learned the lesson of receiving after years of self-perceived 'failure'. Although I had a strong focus on giving, forgiving, and thanksgiving, I was not as good as receiving. I was in the habit of denying myself the gifts that came my way, as if there was an underlying belief that I didn't deserve these good things.

Upon the offer of money from friends or family, I'd say, 'No, don't worry, it's okay. You keep it.' Even though that money was often money returning to me that I had loaned out to them.

So your success and prosperity must be accepted as much as it is given. Some people, though, are more in the habit of taking than giving. They are unbalanced. They suck the energy out of others and usually end up alone, their friends and colleagues long sick and tired of their attitude of taking everything they can without giving back.

Balance is the key. Give well, receive well, and the Game of Life will be played well. Success and prosperity will be yours.

WHITE DIAMOND: THE ATTITUDES OF ABUNDANT LIVING

WHITE DIAMOND PRACTICE—ABUNDANT LIVING

This practice follows on from the green diamond practice, where we discussed the two main sources of knowledge: theoretical and empirical. In the green diamond practice, you learned *what* you need to know about your natural state of being. This practice, *#8 The Attitudes of Abundant Living*, will now focus on gaining empirical knowledge of your natural state of being by learning *how* to apply it.

Return to the list of values in *Table 31: Your Natural State of Values* in the previous practice. There are seventeen values listed in each column. You have already identified your top, high importance values, but this process will work for any and all the values you identify with. We will use *The Attitudes of Abundant Living* to now show you how to experience more of what you want. Let's use humour as an example of a value you want to experience more of.

Giving

One way to experience more humour is to watch a comedy program or attend a live comedy event. But these are usually single episodes during your day and are short-lived. The best way to experience humour on a more permanent basis is to make other people laugh.

Think of the attitude of giving as paying it forward. When you give the gift of laughter to someone, you not only release the humour and joy that is a natural part of who they are, but you also release the natural joy of who you are.

This is your gift to the world.

Forgiving

A past grievance blocks access to your natural state of joy. That void is felt as sadness, anger, resentment, jealousy, and other similar emotions. As long as you are sincere, forgiveness of the person or situation that caused your grievance removes the emotional blockage to your inner joy.

Think of forgiveness as your happy pill. Whenever you feel the pain of a grievance, take a forgiveness pill and you will feel the pain subside and joy filling the void.

This is how you heal yourself and the world.

Thanksgiving

As we've said before, the happiest people in life are the people who are most grateful. Find something to be grateful for, either something that's happened in the past, is happening now, or will happen in the future. Then give thanks to the thing or things that made it possible. It could be a person, or a group of people, a business, the government, or another institution. It could be nature. It could be your mother or father. If you are religious, it could be God.

Think of thanksgiving as the key to unlocking your true self. If you are trapped behind the thoughts, emotions, and instincts of your triune brain, the attitude of gratitude is your key to freedom—the freedom to finally become the person you were born to be.

Receiving

Always receive as well as you give. You've worked hard, so allow yourself to accept the gifts that come your way, especially joy and happiness. You can practice this in three ways:

1. Celebrate your successes—the act of celebrating your wins, no matter how small, opens your mind to accepting the gifts that come your way. Don't take them for granted. Enjoy them!

WHITE DIAMOND: THE ATTITUDES OF ABUNDANT LIVING

2. Believe you deserve the gift of happiness—because if you don't believe you deserve the good things in life, you will mentally block them and fail to appreciate them. Remember, just as success is a habit, so is happiness, and one of those habits is to receive joy with grace and gratitude.
3. Be an empty vessel—a glass half full can only be filled with half as much as an empty glass. Therefore empty the mind of any self-limiting thoughts or beliefs and receive your gifts of joy and happiness to the full.

* * *

When put into practice, the Attitudes of Abundant Living are the surest way to express the real you. You always have something of value to give. You always have time to forgive. You always have something to be grateful for. You always have this moment to receive your gifts of success and to celebrate your wins.

These are the attitudes of Life Leadership.

16 PURPLE DIAMOND: EMPOWER YOUR LIFE

LIFE LEADERSHIP PRACTICE #9

You have now arrived at the final level of your Life Leadership journey, purple diamond. The aim of this level is to attain elite-level knowledge of Life Skill #1–Who, and complete your Life Leadership journey within 3-4 months. The practice of empowering your life is the third in the process of 'Rejuvenating' and moving into Quadrant #1 in the Empowered Living Index.

The core of this practice is unleashing your inner power. In The Diamond Triangle, empowerment is the final building block in your 'I Can' axis, and is now looking like this:

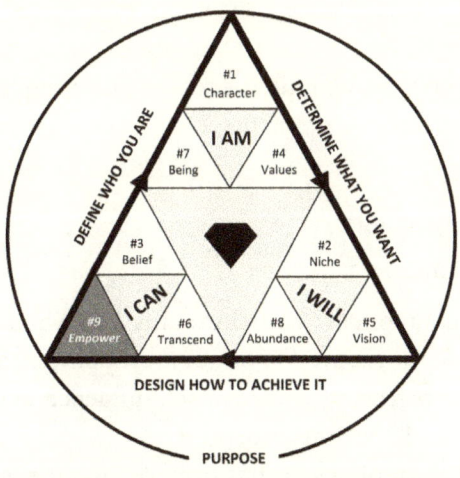

FIGURE 34:   Purple Diamond—Empower

SELF-EMPOWERING BEHAVIOURS

Your 'I Can' is the axis of self-empowerment. It is the axis whereby all Life Leaders maximise their impact, influence, and inspiration. The first building block of this axis is self-empowering thoughts and beliefs, which we discussed in yellow diamond level. The second building block is self-awareness, which we discussed in black diamond level. The final building block is self-empowering behaviours.

The formula for self-empowerment can therefore be written as such:

$$E = T + A + B$$

-> E is self-empowerment

-> T is self-empowering thoughts and beliefs

-> A is self-awareness

-> B is self-empowering behaviours

In this chapter, we will discuss self-empowering behaviours, to which there are three components:

1. Action
2. Responsibility
3. Commitment

All three components constitute any behaviour that is self-empowering. To the extent that one or more of these components is missing in your behaviour, your impact, influence, and inspiration as a Life Leader will be diminished.

The importance of action has been discussed throughout the chapters. Action is the silent 4th Golden Rule—Rule #4: Deliver It. Life Leaders don't wait for things to get better—they actively seek progress and work to implement that progress in all areas of their life. They do this by having a vision, goal setting, and executing their action plan. They know what they want, and they go and get it. They also ensure that they are held accountable to take the action they say they will take, which is usually accomplished with a Life Leadership mentor and coach.

Commitment has also been discussed throughout the book. Commitment to the Life Leadership program, and commitment to your Life Purpose. Commitment is what separates a Life Leader from the rest. It breeds persistence and determination. With it, you stand a great chance of achieving what you set out to achieve. Without it, the road is long and potentially fruitless.

The final component is responsibility. Victor Frankl lamented that the USA was unbalanced because it had a Statue of Liberty on the east coast, but no Statue of Responsibility on the west coast. To him, the USA was too lopsided toward freedom. Without the responsibility that freedom necessitates, people are at risk of derailing. Having freedom is great, but it doesn't mean you can do whatever you like without suffering any consequences.

It is recognised that personal growth and transformation begins when you take personal responsibility for your growth and transformation. To get this far as a Life Leader, you are already taking responsibility for who you are, what you do, why you do it, and how you do it. You are already taking responsibility for your 7 key areas: Family & Relationships, Career & Work, Money & Finances, Health & Wellbeing, Learning & Education, Fun & Adventure, and Spirituality & Ethics. Responsibility is already part of who you are.

But there are two other aspects of responsibility that need to be discussed, failure and success. Taking responsibility for your failures and successes will be the turbo boost to power you across the finish line of Life Leadership.

IT'S UP TO YOU!

RESPONSIBILITY: OWN YOUR FAILURES

It sounds obvious, but only by taking responsibility for your mistakes can you be pro-active and do something to amend the mistakes you have made. Only by taking ownership of the failure are you able to find a solution and move forward.

Just as success is a personal brand, so is failure. Like success, failure must be personally defined. Or more to the point, *re-*defined. Do you see failure as fatal? Do you see failure as an attack to your personal identity, as a weakness? Do you carry the weight of failure with you everywhere you go? Is failure something to be avoided at all costs?

If so, redefining what failure means to you will lighten your load. Life Leaders change their perception of what failure means and embrace it. They don't ignore or deny their failures; they take ownership of them. Doing so enables Life Leaders to 'fail forward' and achieve their personal brand of success. Failure *is* an option because they know the path to success is laid with the stones of failure. But to embrace failure you need a shift in mindset. You need a change in perspective.

In this world of opposites—up/down, left/right, wrong/right, good/bad—we can't have one without the other. Without bad, we can't have the good. Without the negative, we can't have the positive. Without the dark, we can't have the light. This also includes success and failure, victory and defeat. Failure is not the end of the world. Your failures set the scene in which your success can emerge. Your defeats lay the stage upon which your victory can take place.

This may sound contradictory, but you have to *want* to fail in order to succeed. Successful people fail more. Michael Jordan claimed he missed 10,000 shots in his basketball career, and that's why he was a success. Colonel Sanders' recipe for Kentucky Fried Chicken was rejected 1009 times before he found a willing backer. When you fail, you learn what doesn't work. You learn what not to do, which is just as important as knowing what to do. Thomas Edison said he experimented with thousands of different versions of the light bulb before he got it right. His attitude was not of failure, but of discovering 10,000 ways that won't work.

Scientists have actually identified and put a name to this 'failing forward' process, *The Principle of Maximum Error*. This principle states that optimum development occurs when an organism makes the maximum number of mistakes consistent with survival. That is, as long as it doesn't kill you, your mistakes make you stronger. Your failures are actually beneficial to your evolution as a human being!

This attitude of embracing failure as a process for success is encapsulated in the Life Leadership belief that your failures are stepping stones to your success and prosperity.

But if you don't try, you can't succeed. Which is why you need to bypass the barriers preventing you from trying. Which, more often than not, is the fear of failure (or the fear of success). As we have discussed, you only have three natural fears: the fear of abandonment, the fear of falling, and the fear of loud noises. When my daughters were learning to walk at the age of 12 months, they didn't fear failure. They got up, they wobbled, they fell on their butt. But they badly wanted to walk. So they got back up time and time again and eventually learned to keep their balance and put one foot in front of the other. Within months they were running.

If failure is something you fear, you have learned it somewhere in your past. You were a toddler once, and you didn't have that fear. Toddlers teach us lessons in perseverance, ambition, and hard work. When the end result you want is more important than the falling down, then you will overcome your fear of failure.

As John C. Maxwell said:

IT'S UP TO YOU!

When achievers fail, they see it as a momentary event, not a lifelong epidemic. Procrastination is a too high price to pay for fear of failure... Recognize that you will spend much of your life making mistakes. If you can take action and keep making mistakes, you gain experience.[50]

So use your failures to motivate you to succeed. Failure means you've taken a risk. It is therefore something to be proud of—you've tried, you've given it a go. But keep going. Keep trying.

Your success is found at the end of all your failures.

RESPONSIBILITY: OWN YOUR SUCCESS

You've worked hard for your success, so it's your responsibility to take ownership of it. If you don't, someone else will be happy to take it from you and call it their own. So be proud of your role in manifesting your goals. Give others credit where credit is due, but also give yourself credit where it's due. Don't listen to the imposter. Give yourself credit for the effort you've put in. For overcoming your fear of failure and refusing to procrastinate. For having a vison. For setting yourself a mission and mapping an action plan. For taking action when it was necessary.

Neglecting to do so diminishes the value of your achievement. Worse, to the extent that you fail to take ownership of your success, it diminishes your power and your chances of future successes.

This is where Life Leaders stand apart from the crowd. They take a moment to celebrate their victories, no matter how minor or seemingly insignificant. Because no victory is insignificant. Success is self-prescribed, which means it's up to you to prescribe the value each success is worth. That makes it personal. That makes it real.

That makes your life worth celebrating.

---

[50] John C. Maxwell, *Failing Forward: Turning Mistakes into Stepping Stones for Success*, Thomas Nelson, 2000.

PURPLE DIAMOND PRACTICE—ABUNDANT LIVING

The only way out is through, as they say, and fear is a barrier that you must get through if you are to succeed and prosper. Because your success lies on the other side of your fear. That's the lure. But fear can be debilitating. Fear can prevent you from taking action on your dream. In Chapter 2, we mentioned that fear only has power over you if you let it. Whatever fear is stopping you, such as the fear of failure or the fear of success, only you have the power to overcome it. It's your fear. No-one else can do it for you.

But living without fear doesn't meant that fear isn't present. It just means you don't let it control who you are and what you do. Fear will always arise. There will never be a time when it isn't lurking in the back of your mind. But will it stop you from doing what you have to do? Will it stop you from doing what's right? Will it stop you from living your dream?

The fear of failure or success can become a habit like any other habit. Years of fearful thoughts and worries have myelinated the axons in your brain and made them faster and stronger. Such is its constant presence, you've become desensitised to fear and don't even know it's there.

But it's a habit you must break if you are serious about becoming the person you always wanted to become and create the life you deserve. You are bigger than your fears because you are the creator of them. You therefore have the power to break through your fears.

That's why FACE Your Fear is the last Life Leadership Practice:

-> F: Feel It
-> A: Anticipate Difficulties
-> C: Change the Context
-> E: Extract the Truth

IT'S UP TO YOU!

It is my hope and intent that, with this practice, you will be empowered to live the life you want, the way you want, how you want.

To be the Life Leader you were born to be.

* * *

FACE Your Fear

<u>F: Feel It</u>

The problem with fear is that it is a horrible thing to feel. The whole sensation is dislikeable, and our first reaction is to push it away and hope it doesn't come back. What you resist persists, however, including fear. The stronger your resistance, the stronger it pushes back. And it always pushes back.

You cannot conquer your fear if you resist or run away from it. The technique of 'feeling' your fear is a 3-step process that will help diminish your fears and free you to chase your dreams. Next time you sense fear coming to your awareness, follow these steps to prevent it taking control:

1. *Focus* on what the fear feels like.

    Don't judge it. Don't resist it. Just feel it. This 'shines' a light on your fear, and researchers estimate that this alone will reduce its impact by about 40%, which is significant. Your attention is therefore very powerful. Like a thief, fear doesn't like to be noticed, and once it knows you're onto it, it will dash into the shadows and try to escape your glare.

    So focus on your fear and diminish its power.

2. *Name the fear.*

    Is it anxiety? Worry? Procrastination? Dread? Trepidation? Stress? The act of naming the emotion of the fear diminishes its power even further. A thief identified is a thief brought to justice. Just as talking about your problems with someone releases the emotion of the problem and helps you to feel better, naming or putting a label on the fear disempowers its emotional hold on you.

So name the fear and tame it.

3. *Keep your attention* on the fear until it dissolves.

    Because your brain is wired the way it is, the fear will return if you don't keep your eye on it. It's sneaky that way. It waits until you're not looking then takes its opportunity to get swing into action. So be vigilant and keep watch. Take deep breaths. Wait for a few minutes until you feel the emotion of the fear leaving your body and calmness replaces it.

    So keep your attention on the fear and keep it in detention.

The more often you perform this technique, the better you will get at being attentive and the less power fear will have on you.

A: Anticipate Difficulties

To defeat your fear, however, you will need more than just positive thoughts—you will need positive action. As with goal setting, you need to employ both hemispheres of your brain to achieve best outcomes, and part of overcoming fear is to 'think on paper'. This helps you to anticipate any obstacles or barriers you are likely to encounter and thereby create a solution before the problem has even arrived.

You may not have a perfect solution in mind, but even a small improvement of clarity of the path ahead is empowering. Because when you balance a positive mindset with anticipation of the roadblocks ahead, your fears diminish, especially the fear of failure.

IT'S UP TO YOU!

Anticipating difficulties also helps change the way you perceive the future outcome. Fear will have you worry about every conceivable problem and failure and have you thinking of every possible worst scenario. But research shows that anywhere between 80% to 90% of worries don't come true. That means 8-9 out of 10 worries are pointless and even self-sabotaging.

In his memoirs of the Second World War, Winston Churchill mentioned the story of the old man on his deathbed who said he'd had a lot of trouble in his life, most of which never happened.[51]

When we focus on negative outcomes, negative emotions and feelings are born. What you can change, however, is your story. Several days before her netball grandfinal, my daughter was fretting about playing in front of a large group of family and friends who were coming to support her and the team.

'What if I stuff up and we lose?' she said.

'What if you have fun and win?' I replied.

Once you have identified and named the fear getting in the way of your success, use the Wheel of Change belief changing tool to develop a belief or outcome that is more in tune with who you are and what you're capable of achieving. Use it to rewrite the story you keep telling yourself. Write an alternative ending to the one that fear wants you to write.

You have the freedom to envisage your life as you want it to be. Why not make it a story of success and victory? Why not make it an epic story of heroism and adventure?

C: Change the Context

Think of the times when you weren't sure if you were scared or excited. You might have been on a rollercoaster ride, being interviewed for a job, or watching a scary movie at the cinemas.

The reason fear and excitement is sometimes confused is because

---

[51] Winston Churchill, *Memoirs of the Second World War: An Abridgement of the Six Volumes of the Second World War*, Houghton Mifflin, 1959

the neurochemicals released during the fight and flight response and some positive emotional states are the same.

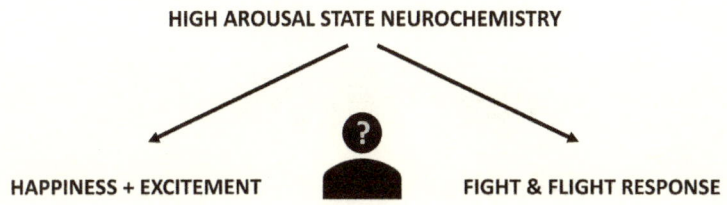

FIGURE 35:   High Arousal State Neurochemistry

But this is good news because the high state of arousal we experience during a fright can be transformed into a more positive experience.

Whenever elite athletes are interviewed just before a major event or tournament, their answers give interesting insight into the human mind. When asked whether they are feeling nervous, they invariably answer, 'No. I'm excited.'

Where others would get nervous and go wobbly at the knees, elite athletes have trained their brains to interpret the enormity of the moment in a positive light. Where amateurs worry about all the possible ways they will lose or fail, elite athletes only focus on the outcome they want—winning.

You too can learn how to decide between a 'rush' and feeling completely terrified. The key is *context*. Research studies into PTSD suggest that context is a significant factor in how people experience fear—you need to perceive and feel that you are *safe*.

The two main areas of the brain associated with the perception of threat are the hippocampus and the pre-frontal cortex. These higher-level centres of your brain process the situational context and evaluate any degree of threat. If the threat level is low, the hippocampus and pre-frontal cortex dampens your fear response. In other words, your higher brain centres reassure your emotional hindbrain that you are safe, and when this happens you can change the experience of fear into enjoyment and excitement.

Table 33: The Pathway of Fear shows how the process works in the triune model of the brain.

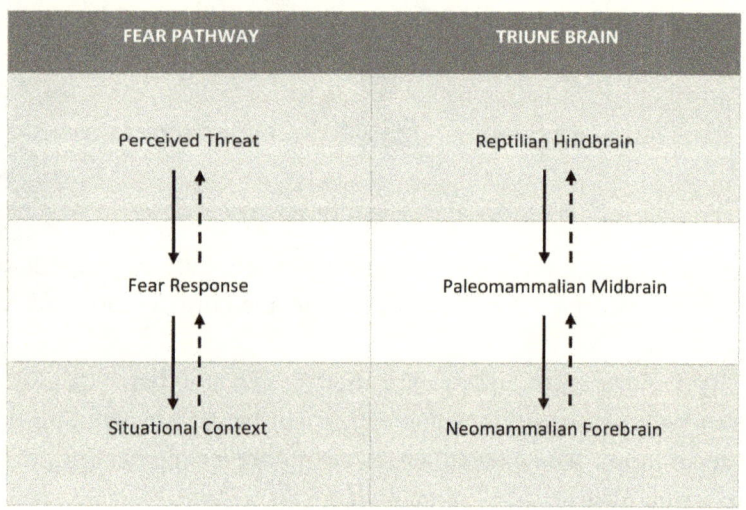

TABLE 33:   The Pathway of Fear

But here is a thought experiment to highlight this point. Imagine being dropped in the middle of the African savanna with no weapons to defend yourself. Suddenly, you hear the roar of a lion close by. Are you scared?

Of course you are. Your brain is telling you you're not in a safe place.

Now imagine you are at the zoo and approaching the lion cage. Are you scared? Probably not, because the lions are behind walls or cages and you know they can't eat you. You have the perception of being safe.

The difference between these two experiences is context, which is perspective. In one you feel safe, and in the other you don't. This is why you can switch from screaming to laughing on a rollercoaster ride or in a horror movie. It's why elite athletes feel excited, not nervous, before a major event.

By changing the context in your mind, you too have this power to change from fright or fear to excitement or enjoyment.

E: Extract the Truth

Your fears can be a tool to unearth the deeper truth of your situation. This is the underlying story you tell yourself through your inner dialogue. The story is verbalised through the mottos you repeat and the beliefs you hold to be true.

For instance, there is an inverse relationship between the fear of failure and self-belief—the more self-belief you have, the more your fear of failure diminishes. You can therefore use your fear of failure (or success) to expose any false beliefs you have about yourself, such as 'I'm not good enough,' or, 'I'll never be a success.'

The fear of failure is but one of many self-created fears. But when faced with fear, take the opportunity to use it as a learning process. You know you have reached Life Leadership mastery when you can examine the causes of your fears without getting sucked into its emotions.

When confronted with fear, unlock the lessons by asking these questions:

-> What is my role in this?

-> What can I do better?

-> What is the big lesson from this situation?

-> What positives can I take from this?

There is always something to learn from your fears. The side-effect is that you grow bigger and your fears diminish.

Don't wallow in victimisation; take the role of a victor. The bigger you become, the smaller your fears become.

It's up to you.

THE LAST WORD

THE DIAMOND TRIANGLE

THE LAST WORD on Life Leadership is, in fact, a reiteration of three words—Define, Determine, Design.

-> Create the ideal version of who you want to be and *define* who you are.

-> Have a clear vision of what you intend to do and *determine* what you want.

-> Empower your life and *design* how to achieve your intentions.

And when you align with the purpose of what you want to be and do, and take action to manifest your dreams, you have the essential factors to Realign, Reconnect, and Rejuvenate and move into Quadrant #1–Desired in the Empowered Living Index and begin *living your being*.

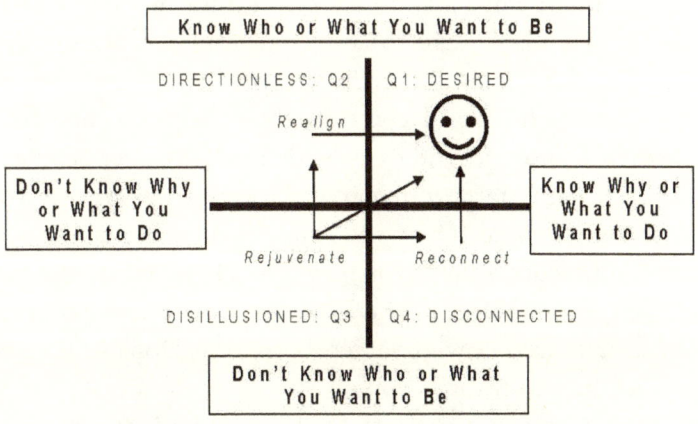

FIGURE 36: The Empowered Living Index—Living Your Being

IT'S UP TO YOU!

Understanding and developing these factors, of course, comes from knowing and embracing the three axes of The Diamond Triangle—I Am, I Will, I Can—which is now shown in its entirety:

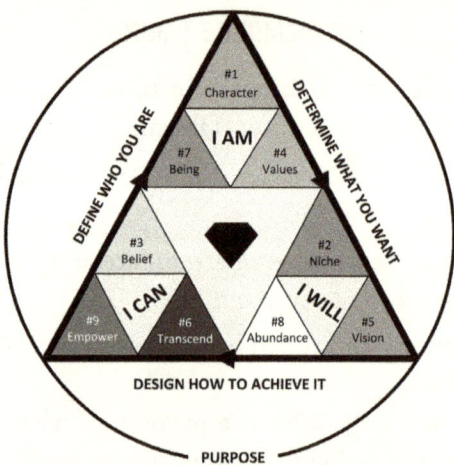

FIGURE 37: The Diamond Triangle—Being, Intent, Power, Purpose

Your being, intent, power, and purpose is the means by which you can manifest your success and prosperity. If the content of this book contributes to your future success, I am delighted to have had some positive impact and I am grateful for the opportunity to help. If you would like to accelerate your Life Leadership journey, I'd be honoured to help you further. I have devoted myself to making the world a better place by helping others fulfil their immense potential and to make themselves better people.

Life Leadership starts with you. If the difference between you and your full potential is how you think, then action is how you bridge the difference. I invite you now to reach out to me and join the growing community of Life Leaders who are committed to helping all of us become who we were born to be. Don't let life pass by you—let life pass through you.

It's now up to you to help make this world a better place by being a better you.

Connect with DoctorZed

Facebook: YNSOB.by.Dr.Scott.Zarcinas
LinkedIn: dr-scott-zarcinas-6572399
Instagram: doctorzed_motivational_speaker
Twitter: @DrScottZarcinas
Website: *scottzarcinas.com*

Growing great people is how you grow a great business!

Are you a leader of a team, involved in a team environment, a business owner, or entrepreneur looking to grow your business?

Ask me how I can help your business grow by growing your people.

E: scott.zarcinas@doctorzed.com
W: scottzarcinas.com/contact

The Life You Want, the Way You Want, How You Want!

Looking for a coach or mentor to help you get direction and take your life to the next level?

Ask me how I can help you maximise your capabilities and reach your fullest potential.

E: scott.zarcinas@doctorzed.com
W: scottzarcinas.com/contact

Book DoctorZed for Your Next Function!
Keynotes • MC • Presentations

scottzarcinas.com/book-doctorzed/

Other Titles by Scott Zarcinas

Your Natural State of Being
by Scott Zarcinas M.D.

ISBN: 978-0-6481315-8-8
eISBN: 978-0-9775969-4-2

DoctorZed Publishing

Available in print and ebook.

'*Your Natural State of Being is refreshing. A tonic to read. Comprehensive and scholarly, it also has so many poetic qualities.*'
~ Roger Rees, Emeritus Professor of Disability Studies and Research, Flinders University

You already have what you are looking for!

Ever wanted the answers to life's deepest questions: Who am I? Why do I do what I do? What am I doing with my life?

Your Natural State of Being helps you answer these questions by getting to the heart of the motivating forces and innermost needs of your life.

But unlike 'quick fix' and 'step-by-step' guides it offers real solutions through the understanding of your true self.

www.scottzarcinas.com/books/your-natural-state-of-being

The Banana Trap: How to Escape a Life of Stress and Finally Break Free by Scott Zarcinas M.D.

ISBN: 978-0-6485726-1-9
eISBN: 978-0-6487107-9-0

DoctorZed Publishing

Available in print and ebook.

Science-based Stress Management Strategies to De-Stress & Prosper

Do you feel overwhelmed and over-stressed? Are you trapped in recurring cycles of worry and frustration? Do you crumble in stressful moments?

Don't worry, everybody has moments of high stress and overwhelm! This guidebook will help you to:

- Feel less overwhelmed and more confident
- Escape The Banana Trap and reclaim your life
- Identify and overcome the different types of stress
- Eliminate stressful habits and increase happiness
- Deal with high-pressure situations and be in control

PLUS develop a long-term strategy to prevent high stress before it occurs.

www.scottzarcinas.com/books/the-banana-trap

www.ingramcontent.com/pod-product-compliance
Lightning Source LLC
Chambersburg PA
CBHW031947080426
42735CB00007B/294